GEMATRIA

GEMATRIA

A Preliminary Investigation of The Cabala

contained in the

Coptic Gnostic Books

and of a similar Gematria in the Greek text of the New Testament

SHOWING THE PRESENCE OF A SYSTEM OF TEACHING BY MEANS OF THE DOCTRINAL SIGNIFICANCE OF NUMBERS, BY WHICH THE HOLY NAMES ARE CLEARLY SEEN TO REPRESENT AEONIAL RELATIONSHIPS WHICH CAN BE CONCEIVED IN A GEOMETRIC SENSE AND ARE CAPABLE OF A TYPICAL EXPRESSION OF THAT ORDER.

BY

FREDERICK BLIGH BOND, F.R.I.B.A.

AND

THOMAS SIMCOX LEA, D.D.

RESEARCH INTO LOST KNOWLEDGE ORGANIZATION
c/o Mrs Janette Jackson
36 College Court, Hammersmith, London W6 9DZ

Distributed by
THORSONS PUBLISHERS LIMITED
Wellingborough, Northamptonshire

This Edition January 1977
Second Impression October 1977

This book is sold subject to the condition that it shall not, by way of trade or otherwise, be lent, re-sold, hired out, or otherwise circulated without the publisher's prior consent in any form of binding or cover other than that in which it is published and without a similar condition including this condition being imposed on the subsequent purchaser.

ISBN 0 7225 0355 5

Printed and bound in Great Britain

EPIGRAPH.

'... numbers are the thoughts of God ... The Divine Wisdom is reflected in the numbers impressed on all things ... the construction of the physical and moral world alike is based on eternal numbers.'

St Augustine

PUBLISHER'S NOTE

The re-publication of *Gematria* marks the fulfilment of a wish held by RILKO since its inception, but it was necessary to choose the right time. This small book by Bligh Bond and Dr T.S. Lea, late Vicar of St Austell, marked the mutual recognition of their independent research into this significant aspect of numbers. Bond had already made his momentous discovery of an ancient science when excavating the ruins of Glastonbury Abbey. While Lea, through his work as a field naturalist, greatly troubled by certain Modernist opinions with regard to the Resurrection, felt that his goal lay 'in some symbolism for the mysteries of the Faith pointing to a mathematical concept underlying them and ultimately to a mathematical "locus" for the miraculous elements they contain.' As a result, they jointly published two small volumes Bond being responsible for the first and Lea the second. Meanwhile, growing interest in the ancient science of numbers, both in Britain and the United States, suggests this as a suitable moment for the re-publication of *Gematria* which has so far been an unsung inspiration to many contemporary scholars, thus adding to RILKO's pleasure in now presenting it as a source book to a new generation which also seeks fresh insight into the perennial philosophy.

Janette Jackson

CONTENTS

	Page
Publisher's Note	vii
Note on the Origins of Gematria	xi
Foreword by Keith Critchlow	xiii
Preface	3
The Method of Gematria	5

Chapter

I	A Brief Outline of the Gematria	7
II	The Existence of the Gnosis	11
III	The Uses of Gematria	18
IV	The Key Applied	24
	Note on Digamma	60
Appendix A	The Number 485	61
B	Of the Square and Circle Contained	63
C	Names of Christ as Multiples of 37	65
D	Schema of the Numbers of Jesus	74
E	The Decree of the First Mystery	80
F	Of the Three Primary Figures	83
G	Cabala of the Cosmos	85
H	The Cube of Light	86
Supplement I	On the Symbolism of Numbers	89
II	On Geometric Truth	95

III The Geometric Cubit as a Basis of Proportion in the Plans of Mediaeval Buildings by Frederick Bligh Bond F.R.I.B.A. (From *The Builder*, Third Series, Vol. XXIII, No. 15, 10 June 1916, pages 249-255. By courtesy of The Royal Institute of British Architects, London.)   97

IV Cephas: The name given by Our Lord to Peter.   111

NOTE ON THE ORIGINS OF GEMATRIA

by Anne Macaulay

Since the time of publishing this book, much progress has been made in tracing the development of the Alphabet (D. Dirringer, *The Alphabet*).

The Alphabet of 22 letters which first emerges historically towards the end of the 2nd millennium B.C. in Semitic hands, was used for numerals as well as letters though the Denary system of numeration may not have been evolved at this early stage. Because of the early usage of the letters as numerals, the practice of Gematria must be associated with this first Alphabet, the ultimate origin of which is unknown.

The suggestion that Gematria may have 'come from a more Eastern source' is still a fashionable view. Much of the ancient wisdom was indeed preserved in the East but the source may have originated elsewhere.

The development in the sixth and fifth centuries B.C. of this system in which 'the principles of Number, Sound and Form (geometry) are connected with each letter' is marked by the extension of the Greek Alphabet in order to have sufficient symbols to accommodate the Denary system of numeration. The Greek person connected with this extension is Semonides of Ceos 556-468 B.C. (Robert Graves *The White Goddess*). The importance of the Greek involvement with Gematria is further attested by the unique Alphabetic usage by the Pythagoreans who used the letters for geometric symbolism (form) as well as sounds and numbers. Like the source of the Alphabet, that of the Pythagorean philosophies and usages is unknown. It is this ancient Greek stream that is the background to the later Greek Gnostic writings.

The use of the 0 or Zero, and the 'Arab' numerals that we use today, are now known to have been used in India and Persia from whence the Arabs obtained the system. Carra de Vaux considers this usage stemmed from a Neoplatonic source (*Everyman's Encyclopaedia*).

In the preface the authors say 'more research will have to be undertaken ...'; from this newer historical perspective the areas for further exploration come into focus. In my view, the study of Gematria can be split into two distinct aspects; 1. The science or gnosis which was concealed in words and numbers; 2. The system of words and numbers itself, i.e., the Alphabet, which went through various stages of development.

Note: Mrs Macaulay has worked on the origins of the Alphabet and is hoping to publish soon.

FOREWORD

A fundamental axiom of the perennial wisdom is that there is an inner determination for all appearances and outward form.

Nowhere more than in the scriptures of the world's religious traditions are we more likely to find this principle of inner and outer better exemplified. Not only are there layers of meaning to each of the scriptures in human, worldly, moral and philosophical dimensions but there is also the inner interpretation of the science of mathematics. The latter is a cosmological expression of the archetypal ideas on which our world depends. This science of mathematics is both qualitative and quantitative and points towards the hidden numerical and geometrical basis of the manifest universe — not as a speculative art but as a profoundly integrative science.

As the aim of Perennial Wisdom is total integration it is useful to appreciate the meaning of the 'passing through' of the different worlds in the process of realization. These psychological realms or 'worlds' have necessary Boundaries or thresholds by which their differences can be known; although they are only aspects of one embracing reality. The passing from one 'world' to another or the crossing of these thresholds of consciousness are matters of precision if the transition is to be made under control and be of lasting benefit to the participant.

Each genuine branch of the Perennial Wisdom has time-tested methods of guiding the sincere seeker through these thresholds in the quest for ultimate integration.

Prayer, in its many forms, is the main instrument for

accomplishing the appropriate stages in psychological integration, and prayer has its aspect of precision.

In the same way that any wise explorer when venturing into a strange terrain would acquire a local guide who knew and had experienced the territory, so a wise seeker after his own psychological integration would seek a psychological guide who had experienced and attained integrated consciousness. The precision of prayer relates directly to the precision of instructions the explorer's guide would give; both are matters of guaranteed safety – if the instructions are followed faithfully.

The Perennial Wisdom has a very ancient maxim which says 'As above so below'. Nobody has serious doubts about the precision of the orbits of the planets of our Solar System and the precise biological rhythms that are set up in all forms of life on planet earth, from waking to sleeping to sowing and harvesting; yet until one considers the inner psychological realm as subject to the same degrees of precision the maxim is relatively inconsequential. As the architecture of above so the architecture of below – so the architecture of the outer, as reflection of the architecture of the inner.

The architectural expression of the Perennial Wisdom resides in the various temples of mankind. Their genuineness is guaranteed by their effectiveness in aiding the same goal of psychological and spiritual integration on a collective scale. The outer forms of these temples vary as much as the different prayer forms of the world, yet the inner content is common – a precise cosmology.

This is cosmology in the original sense of an ordered universe, a creation unfolded from a single all-embracing source or reality. The study of the ratios of this unfoldment has the benefit of indicating similar ratios for the return journey from multiplicity to unity.

As Bond and Lea put it in their own way at the end of this work: 'For all Building, whether of Words, Ideas, Figures, or Material Forms, is founded on fixed proportionals which we have termed Aeonial, and these we study under the name of Geometry.' Architecture, expressed in the symmetry of geometric forms co-related by Measure and Number, has been the interpreter of the Universal Truths as it is the witness of the formative principles which underlie nature and speaks of Immutable Foundations.

This small but intense volume reveals to the sincere seeker a way of discovering the hidden intellect which can become an invaluable companion on the way through the labyrinth of life guaranteeing the unbroken thread of meaning.

Keith Critchlow

PREFACE.

By recovering the Key of the Knowledge (St. Luke xi. 52), and the Mysteries of the Faith (I. Cor. xiii. 2) the Church would greatly increase the strength of her appeal to the thinking man. The authors believe that the Key may be recovered, and the subject-matter of their work already tends to shew that the Apostolic Church possessed a real GNOSIS which made the Faith a great reality and joy to the intelligence, and gave an insight into the nature of the Spiritual powers that were exercised. The Gospel narrative, in its simplicity, is the pure milk of the Word. Christianity was a re-birth of religion (Heb. i. 1, 2) and was preached as to children in the Faith. But that there was reserved for those that had progressed, a more inward revelation, there can indeed be no doubt. And the discovery in the Gematria of the Greek Scriptures of indubitable traces of a coherent and consistent teaching in harmony with the exoteric expression of the Christian dogma and forming a definite link between the theology of the Sacred Books and that wonderful scheme of imagery and symbolism of an architectural or geometrical nature with which the Gnostic Books abound, and which is so evident in Scripture, gives point to that outstanding fact in the story of the life of Jesus, that He was trained as a

Carpenter or Builder (ΤΕΚΤΩΝ), and suggests that behind this natural and outward fact there lies a mystery, namely that He, in His Divine Personality, was the Builder of the Aeons (Heb. i. 2) and that the Knowledge which He gave His Church was the knowledge of those principles by which the worlds were made (Heb. xi. 3).

It should be understood that the authors are fully aware of the immensity and the difficulty of the task that lies ahead in the interpretation of the Teaching discovered, and are conscious of the limitation of their efforts. More research will have to be undertaken, but in the meantime it may be explained that part of the further investigation must be into the meaning of such passages as those in which St. Paul mentions "unspeakable words which it is not lawful (or not possible) for man to utter", and where St. John is bidden to seal up that which the seven thunders uttered. And it is just possible that this revelation has been reserved for these great times in which the Church now struggles to proclaim the Faith.

THE METHOD OF GEMATRIA:

OR ASSOCIATION OF LETTER AND NUMBER.

A BRIEF DESCRIPTION.

About the fifth century B.C. there begin to appear in the Syro-Phoenician centre east of the Mediterranean, traces of a mode of writing in which the letters of the alphabet serve also the purpose of numerals. Though coming from this centre, the origin of the method is not believed to be Phoenician but to be traceable to a more eastern source. From this parent influence two systems are derived. These are the Greek and the Hebrew. Both systems attained a high degree of development about the third century B.C. Both languages are constructed with great skill, and are evidently the work of highly instructed men animated by a clear purpose. Though compiled from older and far less perfect material, they represent something far more than the natural evolution of that material. They shew system, but they also shew peculiarities, sometimes having the appearance of intention, for which no adequate reason has yet been offered. Their alphabets, which are also numerals, exhibit unexplained features, some of which may be described as mysterious. It is scarcely reasonable to suppose that the element of chance has in any appreciable degree entered into their framing. And this is the more unlikely in that there is evidence of a contrary belief among these peoples, who shewed a peculiar reverence for their alphabets, ascribing to each letter its own mystical value, and, to the whole, a body of symbolic teaching in which the principles of Number, Sound, and also Form as connected with each letter, all played their part.

Both the Greek and Hebrew modes of numeration are based on a Denary system: that is to say, one which divides into units, tens, hundreds, etc., but it must be borne in mind that the use of the 0 or Zero was not then known, but was introduced from an Arab source about the third century A.D. Hence the Greek mode of calculation was far more clumsy and laborious.

The Greek Alphabet was perfected at Athens about 400 B.C., when several new signs were added and older compound letters superseded. Other old signs were retained as numerals only. The older Greek numeral system was like the Roman, but even more cumbersome. It is known as the Herodian. (Thompson, *Latin and Greek Palaeography*, 1906, p. 104.)

For the convenience of readers, the Greek numeral alphabet is appended.

Aα	Bβ	Γγ	Δδ	Eε	Ϝ*	Zζ	Hη	Θθ
1	2	3	4	5	6	7	8	9
Iι	Kκ	Λλ	Mμ	Nν	Ξξ	Oo	Ππ	Ϙ*
10	20	30	40	50	60	70	80	90
Pρ	Σσ	Tτ	Υυ	Φφ	Xχ	Ψψ	Ωω	ϡ*
100	200	300	400	500	600	700	800	900

* Ϙ, ϡ—numerals only. For note on Ϝ—the Digamma, see end of Text.

CHAPTER I.

A Brief Outline of the Gematria.

On a top shelf in the study of the 'House Beautiful' there are a couple of Early Christian books which even Mr. Interpreter himself has almost forgotten. Indeed, when a pilgrim asks him, he seems only to be able to say that he really knows practically nothing about their contents.

But Mr. Interpreter is a scribe, made a disciple unto the Kingdom, and will bring forth out of his treasure things new and old, and he has kept his copies of the PISTIS SOPHIA and the BOOKS of IEOU. These are possibly Coptic translations of Greek originals and have many words in Greek, inserted in their nominative cases in the Coptic manner. And both books purport to be Resurrection Discourses of our Lord when He taught His disciples things concerning the Kingdom of Heaven. And though this claim can not be admitted in its entirety, it must not be altogether dismissed, for it cannot have been made without a certain amount of ostensible support, and it may be worth while to investigate what that support may have been.

Now in the New Testament there are several references to the Knowledge and the Mysteries (as in I. Cor. xiii.), which the faithful might learn, as well as to powers which the faithful might exercise and some of these mysteries are still among us and give a hint as to the language in

Investigation of the Cabala.

which they, and probably therefore others, were expressed. Some of these mysteries concern names. It is known that names both in Greek and Hebrew were reckoned by their numeral value. It is, for example, held to be very probable that the celebrated number of the Beast, 666, is that of Nero the Emperor—in the Hebrew נרון קסר* (NRVN QSR = 666).

It was a cipher or code expression according to a well known system which prevailed both in Hebrew and in Greek, and there is good reason for supposing that a great deal of secret information of a political or commercial sort was sent under cover of such a code. But that was not all. The name of the code was ΓΕΜΑΤΡΙΑ or ΓΑΜΕΤΡΙΑ, the latter word being a recognised variant of ΓΕΩΜΕΤΡΙΑ, and it has become clear that this code-method was actually used in these books to record and to memorise geometrical formulae.

It must be remembered that the Arabic numerals were not then in existence, and the letters of the Greek alphabet were used as numerals. The proof of the statement can only be given by the citation of so large a number of instances as to eliminate completely the possibility of chance coincidence. The workings of the mathematical doctrine of chance must be taken into account, but a few illustrative instances may be given. We may recall first the well known example quoted by St. Irenaeus:

A Ω and ΠΕΡΙΣΤΕΡΑ each enumerate at 801, thus identifying the Dove with the First and Last. On this there is a good deal of very striking matter which has recently come to light in the Gematria.

Next we have such geometrical words as ΚΗΦΑΣ— which symbolises the perfect ashlar, or cubic stone, since

$$\mathrm{KH\Phi A\Sigma} = 729 \text{ or } 9 \times 9 \times 9.$$

---

* Written defectively for נרון קיסר.

$A = 1$
$\Omega = 800$
———
801

$\Pi = 80$
$\epsilon = 5$
$\rho = 100$
$\iota = 10$
$\sigma = 200$
$\tau = 300$
$\epsilon = 5$
$\rho = 100$
$\alpha = 1$
———
801

$K = 20$
$\eta = 8$
$\phi = 500$
$\alpha = 1$
$s = 200$
———
729

Outline of the Gematria.   9

Such words as ΘΥΣΙΑΣΤΗΡΙΟΝ—the word habitually employed in Scripture to designate the Altar, and adopted by the early Christians for that purpose, has a like geometrical implication, for

TO ΘΥΣΙΑΣΤΗΡΙΟΝ = 1728 or 12 × 12 × 12, typical of the perfect symmetry of form connected with this feature, the earlier form of the Christian Altar being a cubic one until such time as the reliquaries were attached to it.

The Jewish Holy of Holies, the Debir, (DBIR) is 216 or 6 × 6 × 6. The Greek Sanctuary, the ἉΓΙΑΣΜΑ is 256 or 4 × 4 × 4 × 4, embodying in addition to the Cube a transcendental Fourth measure.

The New Jerusalem of the Apocalypse, figured as a Four-square City, has the number 961 or the square of 31 —Ἡ ΚΑΙΝΗ ἹΕΡΟΥΣΑΛΗΜ = Ὁ ΟΥΡΑΝΟΣ.

With this introduction a specimen of the method in its more intimate application to mathematical principles, as deduced from the old books above referred to, may now be given. It is not pretended that the whole cipher has been decoded, and indeed it would appear that there is at least one other cipher of a different nature to be dealt with in both books, and, generally, there is a great deal more to be done.

There is ΙΕΟΥ himself; the Divinity of Truth—Bishop of Light—by Gematria 485, equated by this method with Ὁ ΠΑΝΑΓΙΟΣ—The All-Holy, a truly remarkable numerical formula—(see Appendix)—whose mathematical powers and possibilities seem to have been regarded as of peculiar importance and as representative of the Creative Principles, as the Gematria of the Nicene Creed may suggest in the phrase

ΦΩΣ ΕΚ ΦΩΤΟΣ = 3395 = 7 × 485.

And on investigation these powers certainly appear unusual, if not indeed unique.

τ = 300
o = 70
——— 370
θ = 9
υ = 400
σ = 200
ι = 10
α = 1
σ = 200
τ = 300
η = 8
ρ = 100
ι = 10
ο = 70
ν = 50
———1358
1728

ד = 4
ב = 2
י = 10
ר = 200
———
216

ἡ = 8
κ = 20
α = 1
ι = 10
ν = 50
η = 8
Ἱ = 10
ε = 5
ρ = 100
ο = 70
υ = 400
σ = 200
α = 1
λ = 30
η = 8
μ = 40
——— 864
961

Ι = 10
Ε = 5
Ο = 70
Υ = 400
———
485

Investigation of the Cabala.

ʹO = 70
π = 80
α = 1
ν = 50
α = 1
γ = 3
ι = 10
ο = 70
s = 200
―― 485

φ = 500
ω = 800
s = 200
――1500

ε = 5
κ = 20
―― 2

φ = 500
ω = 800
τ = 300
ο = 70
s = 200
――1870

3395

M = 40
ε = 5
σ = 200
―― 245

ο = 70
υ = 400
ρ = 100
α = 1
ν = 50
ο = 70
s = 200
―― 891

1136

M = 40
ο = 70
ν = 50
α = 1
s = 200
―― 361

ε = 5
ν = 50
―― 55

τ = 300
ε = 5
τ = 300
ρ = 100
α = 1
δ = 4
ι = 10
―― 720

1136

But there are other numbers which to a certain extent offer a parallel to 485, since they may be employed to give expression to some of the incommensurable relations of geometry in integral terms which represent with approximate exactness such quantities as cannot strictly speaking be expressed by whole figures.

Of this nature are the numbers expressive of the circumferences of circles in relation to their diameters, or enclosing squares.

These, generally speaking, are adjusted upon the basis of the proportionals 22 to 7, and similar conventions exist for the interpretation of such quantities as the arithmetical Roots of Two, Three, Five, Six, and Ten. For example, Heaven is conceived as a circle, and the word ΟΥΡΑΝΟΣ, which is 891 or 11 times the square of Nine, stands for this. The Circle is generated from the Diameter, in this case by convention equal to 284, number of ΘΕΟΣ — GOD, by whom the Heavens were made. And to emphasise the Gematria of these numbers we find that the perimeter of the enclosing square, which is 1136, is the number of ΜΕΣ-ΟΥΡΑΝΟΣ — the Mid-heaven — and of ΜΟΝΑΣ ΕΝ ΤΕΤΡΑΔΙ.

Here then we have a very simple but typical illustration of the Geometric Method, and such as may serve to indicate the lines for further research. Not only the Books of ΙΕΟΥ, but also the Pistis Sophia, appear replete with such instances, but it need hardly be said that that which the writers of these books strove to convey did not rest with the mere consideration of isolated forms, but that they used these as part of a more coherent teaching.

CHAPTER II.

THE EXISTENCE OF THE GNOSIS.

But of the actual or possible theological import of these books or of the whole matter something must needs be said.

The mere existence of the books implies a system, and students of that system, and a belief that the study was worthy of the effort it involved. And it is notorious that there were Graeco-Egyptian schools of mathematical theosophy, and that there was some connection between some Christians and some of these schools, though the results are generally believed to have been neither theologically orthodox nor morally sound, if indeed what may be gleaned of the so-called 'Gnostic remains' be truly representative of their teachings. It is probable however that the doctrines of the mystical school were not, in the best days, committed to writing, but in their decadence some effort was made to preserve from total loss knowledge which was lapsing, or in danger of lapsing, and the books in question may be the witnesses of such an endeavour.

But as the authors of these books are unknown, no personal question can arise, nor can any formal ecclesiastical condemnation of them be found. They must speak for themselves.

Moreover the system of Gematria they contain has

features identical with that discoverable in some of the books of the New Testament.

Tentatively and provisionally the Pistis Sophia may be considered to be the allegorical work of an author who had access to, but had not necessarily mastered, a mathematical theory of the origin of the universe. He names mysteries which he does not always explain. The books of IEOT, which are referred to in the Pistis Sophia as a revelation, are much more advanced. But what the authors do plainly believe is, that certain entities such as the relation of the Square root of Two to Unity, or the area of the Equilateral Triangle to that of the Square on the same base, are aeonial, in the sense of being deeply rooted in the construction of things seen, necessarily involved in all phenomena of symmetric form. And the Church, reading Hebrews i. 2 on Christmas Day, would be in accord with these old authors.

But these relations, however complex and beautiful, are not all that exists. There is a Geometry of the Heavenly Places here indicated—and herein lies the possibility that this work is important. For the present state of science shews a distinct readiness to investigate whether such geometry exists, or what laws govern the unexplored regions in which life, growth, and the dynamic phenomena of nature seem to have their origin.

It is fully in accordance with scientific principles to proceed from the known to the unknown, nor is there anything foreign to this method in the idea that our Lord did actually use the geometry such as any builder might have knowledge of, for the building up of the wisdom of His Church. Even as mere metaphor, this sort of imagery would have its value. How greatly, for example, is the work of the preacher facilitated by the use of the architectonic symbolism of the Bible. But even as metaphor, there may be a better and more real foundation for these building allegories than is at first sight obvious to anyone who seeks to compare things intelligible to the reason with truths of a spiritual nature. Between ideas derived from these two sources the human consciousness seems at all times to have discovered an affinity, and it is hardly too much to say that in the study of the growth of religious and philosophic systems they are found to be inevitably associated. In this respect, the human mind may be attesting subconsciously its recognition of truths which it has been unable to formulate by ordinary mental process or to prove in the terms of ordinary human language. But it is possible that the realities of this correspondence may be conveyed by a language whose terms are those aeonial things, geometry and number, and that the Gnosis of the Apostolic Church had reference to such a system.

The attitude of these early Christian writers, who put forward what purport to be Resurrection Discourses of Jesus in geometrical language and formulae, will have to be appraised most carefully. Geometry is independent of matter; it is aeonial, and by its aid the human mind can almost reach transcendent space. The higher powers of the mind claim kinship with geometry and choose it instinctively as their interpreter for the expression of their ideal conceptions. And it furnishes an avenue to the greater realities beyond human ken.

Now did the Early Christians hold ideas of higher dimensions of space? That is hypothesis only at present. But there is much that makes this hypothesis probable. And it may well be that the mystical geometry which has been imported into their scriptures will itself supply a clue. Thus we should have a locus for miracles, for it is a common characteristic of the miracles of the New Testament that they harmonise with all that can be predicated of action in and from a higher space.

The concept of a higher space is familiar to mathematicians who use its symbols, the higher powers of Number, as a necessary element in their calculations. The idea is familiar also to those who make a thoughtful study of nature and who can find no scope for an explanation of her subtle and mysterious processes within the limits of our physical space. The phenomena of Life—appearing first as a microscopic germ, yet holding within itself the potentiality of growth and infinite reproduction, engender this thought—from what unseen source does it arrive? Modern science is again being compelled to look beyond the visible confines of our space to account for the play of Nature's forces. More than all, in the region of psychology, we touch upon a mysterious field in which the every-day working of natural law seems set at naught. From time to time in history there are recorded outpourings of spiritual force among men, accompanied, as tradition strongly tells us, and more recent chronicles affirm, by the development of strange gifts and powers, endowments of the human will and understanding which enable it to achieve conquests over ordinary or material law.

Such outpourings vary in degree as in kind, from the transient and popular type, which among the simple and unlearned may produce new religious fervour and emotional crisis, with a train of what we may call 'spiritual phenomena'—to the profounder world-movement which is born in chaos, darkness, and the dissolution of older faiths: and for its guidance and for the reconstruction of social and religious order calls forth teachers illuminated with a higher wisdom, inspired by the flame of compassion for the race, and who, by union with the great Realities, have laid hold on the spiritual powers and substances.

Such was the condition of the civilised world when

the Christian religion appeared, and such the character of its apostles. That these men had come into conscious contact with higher realities there can be no doubt. Read the eleventh chapter of the Epistle to the Hebrews —not as a theological treatise or sermon, but as a scientific record of experience—and the conviction arises that their faith was not a mere matter of intellectual and moral assent, but a living and real experience of some order of things transcending the physical, and that they could operate in this higher field.

Prominent among the spiritual possessions with which the Christian religion endowed its converts was a Knowledge of which frequent mention is made by the evangelists and apostles.

The term used to describe this Knowledge is ΓΝΩΣΙΣ, a word implying in this connection a higher sort of knowledge or a deeper wisdom. It would be used both in a general and in a specific sense, but there is little doubt that it had acquired among the later Greeks a very specific meaning in regard to religious teachings.

In the canonical books of the New Testament there are places in which ΓΝΩΣΙΣ is clearly spoken of in the general sense, as in II. Cor. vi. 6; but there are numerous other instances in which the context rather implies some definite teaching which the spiritually enlightened were capable of assimilating.

So intimately is this ΓΝΩΣΙΣ linked with other good gifts such as ΑΛΗΘΕΙΑ and ΣΟΦΙΑ, ΠΙΣΤΙΣ and ΜΥΣΤΗΡΙΑ, that it must be regarded as an essential element in the spiritual inheritance of the disciples. These words are usually accompanied in the text by the definite article, though not always so. Where the word is in the nominative as the subject of a sentence, or a repetition, no specific meaning is to be attached to the article. But in oblique cases its presence is said by grammarians to give a certain emphasis. Such a passage therefore as Luke xi. 52 might be rendered thus, "Woe unto you, lawyers, for ye have taken away the key of *the* Knowledge" (οὐαὶ ὑμῖν τοῖς νομικοῖς, ὅτι ἤρατε τὴν κλεῖδα τῆς γνώσεως). But it is by no means easy to understand the principle on which the translators have dealt with such words as these, since they do not receive equal treatment in all cases. For example, the word ΑΛΗΘΕΙΑ is sometimes given the article in English where it does not appear in the Greek, e.g., II. Thess. ii. 13, where ἐν . . . πίστει ἀληθείας is rendered 'belief of the truth'—and no doubt rightly so (see also I. Tim. ii. 4). But it is noteworthy that the term ΓΝΩΣΙΣ is not accorded the same treatment, and the expression is thus deprived of any specific meaning.

An instance of what appears to be a somewhat arbitrary suppression of the article in connection with the Mysteries and the Knowledge occurs in I. Cor. xiii. 2 (καὶ εἰδῶ τὰ μυστήρια πάντα καὶ πᾶσαν τὴν γνῶσιν)—translated 'and understand all mysteries and all knowledge'. But it can hardly be denied that the words 'τὰ μυστήρια πάντα' convey a very specific meaning and would have done so to the Greeks of the day, who would have connected the words with the religious rites of a secret nature to which they had been accustomed. Similarly πᾶσα ἡ γνῶσις would mean to them a certain body of knowledge associated with those mysteries.

Perhaps however the most cogent argument for the recognition of a genuine ΓΝΩΣΙΣ held by the faithful would be based on the passage in I. Tim. vi. 20, where Timothy, as a bishop, is cautioned by Paul against the oppositions of the False or Pseudonymous Gnosis (ἀντι-θέσεις τῆς ψευδωνύμου γνώσεως) — given in our authorised version as 'the oppositions of science falsely so-called' but amended in the revised version, which reads 'oppositions of the knowledge which is falsely so called'.

That there was a False Gnosis the writings of the Church Fathers themselves testify, and the sectarian teachings of the ΓΝΩΣΤΙΚΟΙ, who represented a number of traditions, or the systems of several schools combined, are held up to condemnation by Epiphanius under this very term, Ἡ Αἵρεσις τῆς ψευδωνύμου γνώσεως.

CHAPTER III.

THE USES OF GEMATRIA.

The inference may hence be drawn that there exists an esoteric teaching dating from great antiquity and finding expression in a harmonised scheme of symbolism in which geometrical and mathematical truth, and their application in architecture and the builder's art play an important part, with a numerical key concealed in this geometrical structure and in the Gematria of language.

Further, that the best elements of this teaching, constituting The True Gnosis, were incorporated into the Christian system of religious teaching, whilst the superstitious accretions were discarded, among those teachings condemned by the Apostle as the Pseudonymous Gnosis being the various speculative offshoots or imitations of the originals, and with them the works of all those who led and supported rival sectarian schools, in fact, most of what is to be gathered from the so-called Gnostic Remains. We may at the same time consider that such works as the Pistis Sophia and the Books of IEOU may or may not contain the genuine Gnosis, but that if they do not, they at least throw very valuable side-lights on the general form in which it was imparted. The correspondences discoverable between the Gematria in the text of these works and that which has been drawn into our Scriptures strengthens their claim to serious attention, whilst the coincidences in the geometrical scheme of symbolism further enhance their importance. The lack of knowledge of these correspondences deprives the modern Churchman of an inner significance or body of teaching undoubtedly subsisting in that which is preserved and handed on to us by the early guardians of the Christian faith—a content of meaning which was evidently considered by them to be vital, and which we cannot afford to disregard.

The Fathers were well acquainted with the system of Gematria, as appears by their own writings, and they could not have failed to realise its intimate connection with the text of the canonical books and the presentation of the Divine story of Creation and Redemption. The key to the system having been lost, it is easy to see a reason for much of the uncertain and inadequate interpretation of Scripture which has marked the subsequent work of its professional exponents.

Some words, some names, are, it is true, capable of a more or less certain interpretation, either on account of a regularity of association, or of a particular clearness of derivation, and an invariability in their form,* but in too many cases the lack of one or other of these qualities gives rise to a doubtfulness of meaning, or of the precise shade of meaning, attributable to them, and where the orthography of a word is in doubt, there, as is well known, controversy may arise and yet worse results may accrue. Some passages of Scripture have become so corrupt through errors, it may be, of transcription, that their very sense has been lost. And as owing to the arbitrary nature of words there is now no rule by which their construction can be positively allied to a particular shade of meaning by any general scientific relation to other words, it must always appear that in any body of teaching such as our

---

* See p. 21.

translations of the sacred books convey, there is an element of hazard affecting the ultimate form and interpretation of those books.

But Number and Geometrical form are aeonially true and constant in their relations, and a system of representation of natural truth having for its vehicle a carefully co-ordinated series of number symbols, in their turn expressive of definite relations of form, would, if it could be practically contrived and interwoven with the text of Scriptural books, have a most conservative effect. Nay more. There are large categories of ideas, mostly of a theological order, which are not capable of clear expression in terms of human language. But it is possible to believe that a mathematical expression can be found for some of these. For these two reasons it is plain that the Fathers and compilers of the text of Scripture, working as they were working, to construct a literary monument which should endure through all future time and defy the destructive tendencies of change and of human error and wilfulness, might in their wisdom seek to incorporate with the variable an invariable, and with the fugitive a permanent, element, by wedding to the letter of the text a Gematria built on aeonial relationships of idea.

And the Letter and the Number would tend to be mutually corrective in case of error, and mutually corroborative where the text is pure. The foreordained relation of number would, in the case of a corruption of text, foreshadow its restoration. This has already been attempted and with some success in regard to the lost Greek of the Pistis Sophia, and it may not be too much to hope that the effect of the same process on doubtful passages of Holy Writ might be found similarly helpful.

But on this matter an apology must at the present stage be tendered for the work is barely yet begun. This apology the benevolent reader will surely understand and

Uses of Gematria.

accept. To work from translations is never satisfactory, and a very big piece of scholarly labour is ahead of anyone who really wishes to do justice to these Gnostic books. A translation into Greek, or reconstruction of the assumed original text, is an essential eventually. But until some *prima facie* case has been made out there would appear no justification for such an arduous work. And, up to the present, Coptic scholars have considered these books as unworthy of their trouble, and have regarded the subject matter as mere magic or astrology.*

The word ΙΗΣΟΥΣ is an example of the more regular and certain order, the spelling being precise in its adherence to this one consistent form throughout the Scriptures. It is alluded to by St. Irenaeus as a name 'of six letters', having an arithmetical significance,† but the good bishop betrays no great knowledge of its meaning.

$$\begin{aligned}
Ι &= 10 \\
Η &= 8 \\
Σ &= 200 \\
Ο &= 70 \\
Υ &= 400 \\
Σ &= 200 \\
\hline
&888
\end{aligned}$$

The name of John is an instance of alternative spelling, the form generally found and usually accepted being ΙΩΑΝΝΗΣ whilst other ancient MSS give ΙΩΑΝΗΣ, and this form is preferred by the editors of some recent editions of the New Testament.

Here then is a case in which the Gematria value of the spelling might be looked to for light, if our theory be correct, and it must be admitted that the name ΙΩΑΝΝΗΣ or ΙΩΑΝΗΣ has an undeniable importance in view of its Divine origin in the Gospel narrative. The numerical value of ΙΩΑΝΗΣ is 1069, a number not apparently related to the general scheme of mystic numbers which

$$\begin{aligned}
Ι &= 10 \\
Ω &= 800 \\
Α &= 1 \\
Ν &= 50 \\
Ν &= 50 \\
Η &= 8 \\
Σ &= 200 \\
\hline
&1119
\end{aligned}$$

$$\begin{aligned}
Ξ &= 60 \\
ι &= 10 \\
σ &= 200 \\
ο &= 70 \\
υ &= 400 \\
θ &= 9 \\
ρ &= 100 \\
ο &= 70 \\
ς &= 200 \\
\hline
&1119
\end{aligned}$$

---

* The 'Magical' Papyri shew traces of a Gematria of which some elements appear to be common to all. But this is no more than saying that the works of charlatans always tend to borrow from the most highly respected sources.

† See W. W. Harvey's St. Irenaeus, Vol. I., p. 332. "Jesus enim nomen alterius linguae existens ad Graecorum numerum transferentes, aliquando quidem episemum esse dicunt sex habens literas: aliquando autem plenitudinem ogdoadum DCCC LXXX VIII numerum habens."

subsists in the writings, but as ΙΩΑΝΝΗΣ, the form generally found and employed by the old scribes, and which is also to be seen in the Coptic MS of the Pistis Sophia, it is 1119, and this it may at once be said is an important number in the mystical geometry of the aeons, and is actually the number of the First Aeon in the Books of ΙΕΟΥ, and is directly connected with the number 634, that of ΒΑΠΤΙΣΜΑ, whilst the ideas of Noah and his ark are connected with the same series. ΞΙΣΟΥΘΡΟΣ (Xisūthrus), the Chaldean Noah, has the number 1119 = Ιωαννης.

β = 2
α = 1
π = 80
τ = 300
ι = 10
σ = 200
μ = 40
α = 1
—
634

M = 40
α = 1
ρ = 100
ι = 10
α = 1
—
152
μ = 40
—
192

A third case is where two different spellings of the same name are found in one work. This is so in St. Luke's Gospel. This Evangelist draws a distinction between the name of the Blessed Virgin—ΜΑΡΙΑΜ—and the other Maries, who are ΜΑΡΙΑ. Here the Gematria is obviously correct for both, as will appear later in the special study which will be offered of these names with that of ΙΗΣΟΥΣ.

The presence in the canonical Scriptures of a Gematria having important elements in common with that discovered in the Coptic Gnostic works, being an undeniable fact, raises issues which cannot be ignored nor put aside by any reverent or thoughtful student. Nor does the fact that the system of Gematria was employed for various secular or common purposes in any way detract from its possibly sacred character. Viewed simply as a language it shares with ordinary language the character of universality, and even its ultimate debasement does not disentitle it to the most respectful examination where its presence is indicated in the Sacred Books. There is a common and familiar element even in the most venerated Names connected with the Gospel narrative. ΙΗΣΟΥΣ and ΙΩΑΝΝΗΣ are both ordinary names, borne by vast multitudes of ordinary people, and yet what a world of significance is implied in St. Luke's narrative of the Giving of these names by the angel. So that in these, as in the numbers of the Gematria, we are warranted in assuming a special, as well as a general significance, and in regard to the names we have mentioned, it is not possible for any believer in the Gospel story to put aside the plain statement as to the Divine origin and intention of these names. They are, indeed, pivotal in the whole doctrinal scheme of the Christian religion, and to doubt this would be to raise grave theological issues. Nor is it tolerable to suppose that any element of the puerile or the fantastic could have been admitted knowingly by the writers of the Gospels in connection with matters of the profoundest import for the whole of humanity. The proposition is unthinkable. Yet here is the system and it is inseparable from the text. We have then a possible alternative in regarding it. We may view it either as a vehicle for Inspiration, or as a contrivance for teaching of the mysteries of the Faith, a product of human skill and learning having a most pious and serious aim. If the latter, we need not be daunted by the fact that there are many fallible and imperfect conclusions of human science linked with the sacred numbers, any more than the fact of the name ΙΗΣΟΤΣ being borne by ordinary and fallible persons need affect our mental estimate of the Divinity of our Lord.

But we shall be seeking for traces of aeonial truth and a foundation of immutable things in these Sacred numbers and for their interpretation in a theological sense, being well assured that a method of interpretation must exist, for it is equally inconceivable that a Book framed for the guidance and enlightenment of the whole human race should contain statements of an unintelligible nature, or to which the key has been permanently lost.

CHAPTER IV.

THE KEY APPLIED.

It is now proposed to offer the reader some further proof of the presence of a coherent scheme of Gematria of a geometrical nature in the New Testament which will serve to show the great importance of the doctrinal meaning to be associated with number, or capable of being so associated, and the peculiar value and precision of the method of numbers for this purpose. Reference will be made also to the Gnostic books, but the main argument and illustrations will be drawn from the canonical Scriptures.

The number EIGHT, which has been called the Dominical number, is found everywhere symbolically employed to convey the idea of Salvation, Perfecting, and Regeneration, from the Company of Noah, onwards through the Bible, and is nowhere more emphasised than in the name of our Lord, which teaches the doctrine of the perfected Humanity in the 888 of ΙΗΣΟΥΣ. This, there can be little doubt, is the mystery to which Irenaeus alludes when he describes the numbering of the name of Jesus. To this moral or spiritual perfection the figure of the cube is allied on the geometric side—and our Lord seems to give His sanction to this teaching when He gives to Peter the name ΚΗΦΑΣ. This suggestion of perfectness in the number Eight is reflected in the constitution of the Greek alphabet with its three Ogdoads* of units, tens, and hundreds—the final Ω which, with the A, takes its place in our Christian arithmology, being 800—in Gematria ΚΥΡΙΟΣ—Lord—the leading epithet of Christ and in the Old Testament of God. The 800 of ΚΥΡΙΟΣ is found in antithesis to the 600 of ΚΟΣΜΟΣ—the World; just as the 888 of ΙΗΣΟΥΣ is in a yet more marked degree contrasted with the 666 of the Beast of the Apocalypse, whose number emphasises the qualities of incompleteness and materiality.

With the idea of a spiritual revelation is associated Light, and the Divine significance of Light is clearly apparent in the number symbolism of the Scriptures as well as in the Gnostic books.

The number of Light—ΦΩΣ—is 1500. It is the Robe of the Lord—ΕΝΔΥΜΑ ΚΥΡΙΟΥ. ΕΝΔΥΜΑ—500—is one of the many mystical words, or words appertaining to the mystery-religions, used by St. Paul.

In the Pistis Sophia Jesus has three of these robes of light, and the number of the word ΕΝΔΥΜΑΤΑ—801— is again that of the A and Ω, and of the ΠΕΡΙΣΤΕΡΑ. And the three ΕΝΔΥΜΑΤΑ are 3 × 500 = 1500 which is the number of Light (ΨΩΣ).

801 is three times 267, the number of the Kingdom— Η ΒΑΣΙΛΕΙΑ.

Ten times this number is 2670—ΚΥΡΙΟΣ ΦΩΤΟΣ, Lord of Light, or, as applied to Christ, ΤΟ ΦΩΣ ΚΟΣΜΟΥ—The Light of the World, who is also ʹΗ ΔΥΝΑΜΙΣ ΜΕΓΑΛΗ ΦΩΤΟΣ (2670)—The Great Power of Light, which descends upon the Lord in the Pistis Sophia. This is also the number of the Church of Jesus Christ— ʹΗ ΕΚΚΛΗΣΙΑ ΙΗΣΟΥ ΧΡΙΣΤΟΥ. Incidentally we may here point out that the number of the Great Power

---

* See figure of Cephas.

(Ἡ ΔΥΝΑΜΙΣ ΜΕΓΑΛΗ)—the title so blasphemously claimed by Simon Magus,* is 800 = ΚΥΡΙΟΣ.

Light, though really threefold, has traditionally also a sevenfold nature. The emanations of the Divine Essence are figured in the Apocalypse as Seven Lamps, which are the Seven Spirits of God, and the seven stars which are the Angels of the Seven Churches. In the scheme of geometric representation, the first emanation from, or manifestation of, the Absolute, in the series we are now considering, is figured as a Cube developed from an original point, which is one of its angles, and this is portrayed in its visible aspect of symmetry as a Hexagon with six internal lines radiating from the centre.

Theoretically there is a seventh radius but never more than six are visible because the seventh approaches the eye and unites the central visible point with the eighth point lying exactly behind it.

The Six outward points, with their connecting lines, represent the Kosmos, or manifestation of the Divine Power, and the seventh, the central point, is the Divine Source, the revelation of God to man.

But the eighth or invisible original is required to complete the figure of the cube, which is only apprehended by the higher reason.

The Six again may be held to represent the periods of Creation and the seventh point, the Sabbath rest of God.

---

* Simon Magus as Σιμων ὁ Μαγος has the number of the Omnipotence—Ἡ Αυτοδυναμις, which follows logically from his self-chosen title of Ἡ Δυναμις Μεγαλη = 800 = Κυριος.

Ελυμας presents the number 676, a very favourite cabalistic number, being the square of the tetragrammaton IHVH or 26, and as ὁ Ελυμας he is a double Λογος being 2 × 373 or 746, the Gnostic Χαραγμα.

Σκευας—another of these magicians (Sceva in our translation) is probably only a Greek nickname—the Reverend 'Make-up'.

The Key Applied. 27

But the perfect, or New, Creation is symbolised by the Cube, for a true knowledge of which a sense beyond that of mere physical vision is required. By this the presence of the seventh ray is revealed and the Eight points are manifest in their true relation. Thus from One are seen to proceed Seven and the Seven are connected with the parent One by rays or lines of Three several lengths (or which are now seen to be of three several lengths), whereas in the flat representation only six were seen, and they were apparently of equal length.*

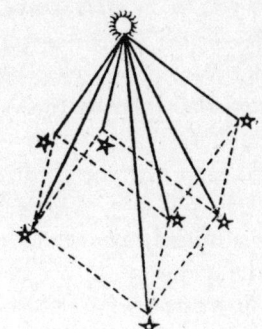

Now we are in the presence of three geometrical entities which by their joint operation determine the form of the Cube, and these are first, the length of its side which is figured as 100—the basic number in the Denary system (far older than the decimal notation), on which the whole of the Gematria may be said to be built. In the Appendix the Cube of Light and its special Gematria will be found fully described.†

There are, as will readily be seen, three rays of this first order emanating from any one point in the cube, and connecting that point with the three lying nearest to it in the cube. Secondly there are to be seen three more connecting lines which are the diagonals on the square sides

---

* cf. Pistis Sophia, Schwartze, p. 6. "Atque erat lux tota secum invicem. Erat tribus modis, atque erat alter praestantior altero, infinito modo. Secundus, qui in medio, praestabat primo inferiori (sc. loco posito), et tertius, superior istis omnibus, praestabat secundo inferiori. Et primus splendor positus est infra haec omnia, similis luci, quae venit super Iesum, antequam adscendit in caela, et aequalis sibi erat valde quoad suum lumen. Atque tres modi luminis erant variae lucis et erant vario τυπῳ aliis aliis praestantibus infinito modo.

† See Appendix H.

of the cube, linking the first point with the three next in order of remoteness, and these lines, on the scale now determined, measure each 100 × √2, or 141·42 — their total, 424·26, being integrally expressed as 424 or 425 by substituting unity for the fraction. Finally, there is the One ray leading diametrically across the cube to the opposite point, and the measure of this is 100 × √3, or 173·205. Call this 173. Thus we have for the total of the Seven rays the sum 300 + 424·5 + 173, which is 897 or 898 and may with equal propriety be taken as either, as the actual figure is halfway between. Hence we find in Gematria that whereas 897 gives ΑΙ ζ' ΕΝ ΤΗ ΑΣΙΑ ΕΚΚΛΗΣΙΑΙ, 898 is the number by Gematria of ΟΙ ζ' ΑΣΤΕΡΕΣ, the seven stars or rays which are the angels of the seven Churches.

In the three incommensurable orders of magnitude derived from the measures of the cube we have clearly a very suggestive parallel to the description in the Pistis Sophia of the three kinds of Light in the Lord's ἐνδυμα, which we are told vary in the quality of their beams (variae lucis) and in the incommensurable nature of their proportions (vario τυπῳ aliis aliis praestantibus infinito modo).

What are the authors of this old book trying to tell us? Let us assume that they really mean something — that they have a rational idea which they are trying to express. With this assumption let us then endeavour to see what sort of parallel modern science can offer to the interpretation we have placed upon the 'seven rays' and the three cardinal measures of the Cube.

Those who have studied the physics of Light will know that the reputed Seven colours of the spectrum are really Three, and that the blending of these three produce the effect of Seven. There are three primary sensations of colour, and three only, the Red, the Green and the

Violet-blue. And these each occupy a certain part of the field, indefinite as to its boundaries, but having an acme of intensity at or near the centre of each section. Near the centre of the spectrum, at a point where the purest green is observed, is the position of one of the fixed lines of colour known as Frauenhofer's E line. There are other such lines, lettered A to H, distributed over the field, and these are measured according to their wavelength, in inverse order to their frequency, and the lengths are given in what are called tenth-metres (see Ganot's Physics).

The whole series of light-rays comprises those whose wave-length varies from a little more than 7600 tenth-metres in the extreme Red to a little less than 3900 in the extreme Violet—altogether about an octave of light. Now if we take our Green ray at about line E or 5270 in measure, then our series must be as follows:—

$$\text{Red } 7453 \ldots \text{ or } 5270 \times \sqrt{2}$$
$$\text{Green } 5270$$
$$\text{Violet } 4302 \ldots \text{ or } 7453 \times \frac{1}{\sqrt{3}}$$

and this is remarkable, because 7453 brings us to the intense Red close to Frauenhofer's A line (7604) and between it and B, whilst 4302 for the Violet brings us to the point of the most intense deep Blue, and practically on to Frauenhofer's line G, which is 4307.

We must be content to leave our instructed readers to judge as to the real nature of so striking an approximation. If, on further investigation, the parallel appears based on undeniable physical fact, then a few more such instances may go far to rehabilitate the lost wisdom of Antiquity. And if it be true that the data of the colour-scale—which are derived from molecular motions—are indeed founded upon harmonics whose source is not, as in the case of Sound and other physical measure, based upon the interaction of forces having whole-number proportionals, but upon those mysterious entities, the Roots of Two and Three, then we are face to face with a condition pointing to a genesis of motion in a region of space unknown to us, and wherein the dynamic laws operate in a relation quite unfamiliar. It looks as if a fourth and *interior* dimension must be assumed, and is this not precisely what some physicists say of the Atom, that it must possess some substance in a fourth direction?

THE METACUBES.

A beautiful extension of this geometrical scheme and one which arrests the attention on account of its scope, precision, and fidelity to the Christian dogma is discovered in the following.

The first Cube, which is the Cube of One, presents, in the diagram, seven points or angles at which the edges meet, but the second, which is the cube of Two, exhibits Nineteen such points, and the third, the cube of Three, shews Thirty-seven. These are of course the differences of the first three cubes; viz., 8 − 1, 27 − 8, and 64 − 27. If instead of drawing the outlines of the cubes, we indicate these angles by clusters of points, the resulting figures may be termed Metacubes, as they register these cube-differences, which are of prime importance in the Gematria (see p. 32).

Now when we come to analyse the Names, Titles, or Epithets of Our Lord in the Scriptures, the extraordinary fact becomes apparent that in an altogether disproportionately large number of cases, these names, etc., are by Gematria, multiples of 37. For example, there is the word ΘΕΟΤΗΣ—Deity or Divinity (Godhead), by Gematria 592 or 37 × 16, which added to ΙΗΣΟΥΣ—888, gives us 1480, the number of ΧΡΙΣΤΟΣ. ΙΗΣΟΥΣ is 37 × 24, and ΧΡΙΣΤΟΣ, 37 × 40. Note again that they are all divisible by Eight.

ΙΗΣΟΥΣ ΧΡΙΣΤΟΣ is 2368 or 37 × 64, and 64 is the number of ΑΛΗΘΕΙΑ. And it has as a Gematria equivalent the following among many others.

Ὁ ΘΕΟΣ ΤΩΝ ΘΕΩΝ.
Ὁ ΑΓΑΘΟΣ ΤΩΝ ΑΓΑΘΩΝ.
Ὁ ἉΓΙΟΣ ΤΩΝ ἉΓΙΩΝ.

For ΙΗΣΟΥΣ 888 there are numerical equivalents in ΛΟΓΟΣ ΕΣΤΙ, Ἡ ΖΩΗ ΕΙΜΙ and numerous others. For ΧΡΙΣΤΟΣ an alternative on the number 1480 appears in ὙΙΟΣ ΚΥΡΙΟΣ and another in Ἡ ΘΕΟΤΗΣ ὙΙΟΥ—the Divinity of the Son, whilst Ἡ ἉΓΙΩΣΥΝΗ—Holiness (Ep. Rom. i. 4) has the same number, as has also the name given to the Lord's Table by the early Christians —Ἡ ΤΡΑΠΕΖΑ ΜΥΣΤΙΚΗ.

As ὝΠΑΡΞΙΣ—Substance, or real possession, His number is 851 or 37 × 23 as Ὁ ἉΓΙΟΣ ΙΣΡΑΗΛ it is 703 or 19 × 37. Ἡ ΣΩΤΗΡΙΑ ΙΣΡΑΗΛ is 1776 or 2 × 888, and ΤΟ ΣΩΤΗΡΙΟΝ ΙΣΡΑΗΛ, the other form, is 2257 or 37 × 61, on which also we find ΚΙΒΩΤΟΣ ΝΩΕ—a remarkable parallel. But it were tedious here to enumerate even a small part of these. A fuller list is given in the Appendix.

We have noted the fact that ΘΕΟΤΗΣ—Divinity = 592, added to the 888 of ΙΗΣΟΥΣ, give us 1480 = ΧΡΙΣΤΟΣ, but even more striking is the fact that when all three are added together we have 2960 which is ὙΙΟΣ ΤΟΥ ΑΝΘΡΩΠΟΥ—Son of Man, the term so often employed by our Lord in speaking of Himself. The component words are multiples of Eight, the Dominical number, as well as of 37, and the number of ΙΗΣΟΥΣ ΧΡΙΣΤΟΣ is 2368 or 37 × 64. The latter number is the

Square of Eight symbolising a yet greater perfection from the fact that it is also a Cube number. And it contains the number of the Truth—ΑΛΗΘΕΙΑ = 64.

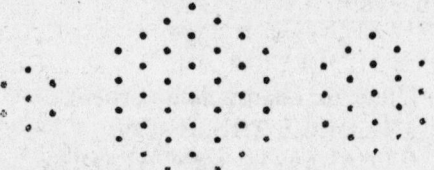

Sixty-four is the cube of Four, but the cube of Three will give us graphically this number of points, in the intersections of the lines which are the boundaries of its component cubes.

Now, of these 64 points, which may be considered to represent the truth in its completeness, only a certain number can be apprehended by the sight. Thirty-seven is the total visible at any one time. The number 37 may thus imply the Manifestation in visible form to Man of God's ΑΛΗΘΕΙΑ. Eight are within the Cube, and the whole number of surface points is 56, and 56 × 37 or 2072 the number of 'Η ΓΕΩΜΕΤΡΙΑ ΚΟΣΜΟΥ, etc.

Now as 37 is to 64—the revealed Truth, to the unmanifest—so is 888, the number of Jesus, to 1536. And 1536 is 'Η ΓΕΩΜΕΤΡΙΑ ΑΛΗΘΕΙΑΣ.

Yet more astonishing is the result when we go back to the second cube-difference, namely 19, which is 27 minus 8. Just as 37, the third cube-difference, is the basic number of the Christos series of names, so is 19 that of the names and titles of the Virgin Mary.

Again, we may depict 19 as the number of visible points on the surface of the Cube of Two, in its symmetric aspect, the true total being 26. Now, as

19 : 37 :: 456 : 888.

And 456 is the number of ΜΗΤΗΡ—the Mother.

The Key Applied.

456 then is the number of visible points, each counted as 24, whilst the invisible counterpart is 8 × 24, or 192, the number of MAPIAM, so that the whole number is that of MAPIAM MHTHP — Mary the Mother. MAPIAM is the spelling of the name chosen by St. Luke, who, curiously enough, makes a distinction between her and the other Maries, who are given the number 152 (MAPIA), and 152 is 8 × 19.

Lastly, let us compare the full numbers 37 × 64 and 19 × 64.

$$19 \times 64 \qquad 37 \times 64$$
$$1216 \qquad\qquad 2368$$

Ἡ Μητηρ ἡ Θεοτοκος.   Ἰησους Χριστος.

And if each of the 64 cubes in the cube of 4 be reckoned as 40, then the whole cube will be 2560 or 10 times the fourth power of Four, which is the sum of 2368 and 192 (Ιησους Χριστος and Μαριαμ), then the number of the visible points will be 37 × 40 or 1480 = ΧΡΙΣΤΟΣ, whilst the concealed number will be 27 × 40 or 1080 the number of ΤΟ ἉΓΙΟΝ ΠΝΕΥΜΑ — the Holy Ghost. 2560 is Ὁ ΤΟΠΟΣ ΤΟΥ ΚΥΡΙΟΥ,* so this may be analysed either as a geometrical Fourth power, typical of the Higher or Transcendental World; or on the theological side as the union of two principles, of which the two above-given instances are expressive. It will also be seen from the foregoing that

ΙΗΣΟΥΣ = 888
ΜΑΡΙΑΜ = 192
———
together give 1080 = ΤΟ ἉΓΙΟΝ ΠΝΕΥΜΑ.

In this connection the following may be regarded as worthy of note.

Twice 888, the number of Jesus, is 1776, for which, in

---
* Or ὁ νους του κυριου.

the Biblical Gematria, we find the expression 'Η ΣΩΤΗΡΙΑ ΙΣΡΑΗΛ. There is some reason to think that the doctrine of the Holy Trinity is concealed in the phrase, for it represents the three Godheads, being 3 × 592, or ΘΕΟΤΗΣ. And the parallels in the Gematria are not a little astonishing; as witness—

$$\begin{array}{ll} \text{ΘΕΟΤΗΣ} = 592 & \text{ΠΑΤΗΡ} = 489 \\ \text{ΑΓΙΟΤΗΣ} = 592 & \text{ΥΙΟΣ} = 680 \\ \text{ΑΓΑΘΟΤΗΣ} = 592 & και\ \text{ΠΝΕΥΜΑ} = 607 \\ \hline 1776 & 1776 \end{array}$$

$$\begin{array}{l} \text{Ο ΘΕΟΣ} = 354 \\ \text{Η ΜΗΤΗΡ} = 464 \\ \text{Ο ΙΗΣΟΥΣ} = 958 \\ \hline 1776 \end{array}$$

ΙΩΑΝΝΗΣ. 1119.   The number 1119 is important as being that of the name of the Baptist, mystically communicated by the Angel to Zacharias.

The name, among the Hebrews, was a common one and means 'Jah is Gracious'. We are not, as in the case of the name ΙΗΣΟΥΣ, bound to regard the particular mode of spelling as invariable, but as ΙΩΑΝΝΗΣ—1119 it plainly has a mystical teaching in connection with the Baptism of Jesus containing as it does the threefold potency of the ΛΟΓΟΣ (1119 = 3 × 373 ΛΟΓΟΣ) and herein we may trace a foreshadowing of the triple manifestation of God's Essence at the Baptism. And the name ΙΩΑΝΝΗΣ is linked to that of Jesus, since by Gematria ΟΝΟΜΑ ΙΗΣΟΥΣ is 1119,* and this again is

---

* The number of the Metacube, Ονομα μετακυβον, see Appendix D.

The Key Applied.

ΕΚΚΛΗΣΙΑ = 294
Ὁ ΠΕΤΡΟΣ = 825
———
1119

(The Church and her Foundation).

Light and Baptism were two ideas peculiarly associated in the teaching of the early Church. ΙΕΟΥ in the Gnostic Books is the 'Bishop of Light'*, and his number is 485. If to this number we add 634, the number of ΒΑΠΤΙΣΜΑ, we have 1119. But this is not a mere addition of two chance numbers. It is the union of two geometrical aeons. Take 485 in this illustration as the area of an equilateral triangle. Set that triangle within the square raised on the same base and the area of the triangle being 485, that of the square will be 1119, their difference being 634. ΙΩΑΝΝΗΣ is related to the Power of Light precisely as the Logos is, by geometry, related to the Aeon. For each pair of words is expressive of the relation of the Square to the Triangular area, thus, ΙΩΑΝΝΗΣ—1119 is the area of an equilateral triangle on the same base as the square 2583—which is Ἡ ΔΥΝΑΜΙΣ ΦΩΤΟΣ—the Power of Light, and ΛΟΓΟΣ 373 is similarly related to ΑΙΩΝ 861.

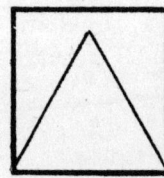

Sq. area = 1119
Triangle = 485
Difference = 634

Other parallels may be detected in the numeration 1119 as Αἰ ζ' λυχνιαι—The Seven Lamps, or Ἥλιος Α.Ω. In connection with the latter it may be noted that both SS. John are solstitial Saints.

———
* The 'Cube' of Light, see Appendix H.

ΦΩΝΗ.   The Voice or Sound is the Power that brings
1358.   the Worlds into manifestation. The Acts of
Creation are rendered thus in Scripture '*And
GOD said*'. And it is the Word, the ΛΟΓΟΣ of God
which is the Builder of the Aeons. ΦΩΝΗ, then, is the
Power of which ΛΟΓΟΣ is the articulate manifestation.

ΦΩΝΗ has the number 1358 which is also the number
of the Altar—Θυσιαστηριον: also of the Gnosis as:—

ΕΠΙΓΝΩΣΙΣ = Perfect Knowledge,
Ἡ ΜΕΓΑΛΗ ΓΝΩΣΙΣ = The Great Knowledge.
ΓΝΩΣΙΣ ΚΑΙ ΑΛΗΘΕΙΑ = Knowledge and Truth.

ΦΩΣ—Light, the First Creation of God by the power
of His Word, has the number 1500. It is by these two
principles that GOD is manifested and the two form a
duplicate Pleroma or Fulness, which is the Treasury of
Light.

1358 + 1500 = 2858 = 2 × 1429,
and 1429 = ΤΟ ΠΛΗΡΩΜΑ—The Fulness.
       = ΘΗΣΑΥΡΟΣ ΦΩΤΟΣ—Treasury of
                       Light.*

Ἡ ΦΩΝΗ ΒΟΩΝΤΟΣ—The Voice of One crying—
is again 2858, and is the sum of the ΛΟΓΟΣ—373,
ΙΩΑΝΝΗΣ—1119, and Ἡ ΦΩΝΗ—1366.

ΧΡΙΣΤΟΣ—1480, and ΒΑΠΤΙΣΜΑ—634, unite to
make 2114 which is the number of the Way of the Lord
—ὉΔΟΣ ΤΟΥ ΚΥΡΙΟΥ. And as ΦΩΝΗ ΕΝ ΕΡΗΜΩ
the Voice in the Wilderness is 2366, identical by Gematria with the Voice of the Lord—Ἡ ΦΩΝΗ ΚΥΡΙΟΥ,
and with Jesus the Saviour—ΙΗΣΟΥΣ Ὁ ΣΩΤΗΡ. If to
this 2366 be added the number of ΒΑΠΤΙΣΜΑ—634,
there appears the number of the Fulness of Christ, the
ΠΛΗΡΩΜΑ ΧΡΙΣΤΟΥ—2739, which is also that of the

---

* See both Gnostic Books.

The Key Applied.

High Priest of God—the ΜΕΓΑΣ ἹΕΡΕΥΣ ΤΟΥ ΚΥΡΙΟΥ, and by the addition of unity becomes 2740—ἹΕΡΕΥΣ ΚΑΤΑ ΤΗΝ ΤΑΞΙΝ ΜΕΛΧΙΣΕΔΕΚ—Priest after the order of Melchisedek.

He who cries in the Wilderness—Ὁ ΒΟΩΝ ΕΝ ΕΡΗΜΩ—is 2000, and this is the sum of Ἡ ΦΩΝΗ—1366, and ΒΑΠΤΙΣΜΑ—634.

Ἡ ΦΩΝΗ and Ὁ ΒΟΩΝ—1366 + 992, are together 2358, which is ΦΩΝΗ ΚΥΡΙΟΥ. Ἡ ὉΔΟΣ and Ὁ ΒΟΩΝ—352 + 992 are together 1344 = ὉΔΟΣ ΚΥΡΙΟΥ.

There is here a perfect arithmetical correspondence which no mere juggling with numbers will explain. The several words, single and combined, are, as it were, members of one body, the soul animating which is a doctrinal significance consistently pervading the whole.

Take the next passage. In Luke iii. 3 we find the expression 'Baptism of Repentance'. Now Ἡ ΜΕΤΑΝΟΙΑ—Repentance—has the number 485, which, as already shewn, is that of IEOU, the Greek Tetragrammaton of the Coptic Gnostic books, 'Bishop of Light', and Divinity of Truth. And 485 is the complement of 634—ΒΑΠΤΙΣΜΑ—in the number of the first Aeon of those Books, which is 1119, the number of the Threefold ΛΟΓΟΣ and of ΙΩΑΝΝΗΣ. In this, then, we have another Cabala of 1119, teaching that the name of John signifies Baptism and Repentance.

Again in the following verse occur the words 'Make His paths straight'. The word for 'path' is ΤΡΙΒΟΣ, and the paths of the Lord are therefore ΤΡΙΒΟΙ ΚΥΡΙΟΥ = 1492, which is not only the value of the text-word ΒΟΩΝΤΟΣ—of One Crying—but is the sum of 1119 ΙΩΑΝΝΗΣ, and 373 ΛΟΓΟΣ—and hence a quadruple ΛΟΓΟΣ (373 × 4 = 1492). This most interesting number is represented in Gematria by the epithet of Our Lord found in I. Cor. xv. 45—the Last Adam—Ὁ

ΕΣΧΑΤΟΣ ΑΔΑΜ, the Gemellus Sōtēr of Schwartze's translation, now restored as Ὁ ΔΙΣΩΤΗΡ = 1492. The parallelism of ideas is very obvious.

But however remarkable the arithmetical correspondence shewn in the above examples, it would be of inferior importance unless the numbers themselves had some intrinsic meaning derived from their essential nature. What is really of importance is the fact that all these numbers are of one order *and can be expressed as a mathematical or algebraical series,* representative of fundamental principles in the geometry of the Aeons. What this series is we shall endeavour to make clear. It is concerned with the successive operation of the Generative Power of the number Three, arithmetically symbolised by certain whole numbers chosen to represent the irrational quantities or surds which denote the triangular and other kindred measures in which the root of three is to be traced. Thus, for example, the aeonial relation of the side of an equilateral triangle to its altitude is as 1000 to 866 +, and that of the breadth of a rhombus of two equilateral triangles to its length, is as 1000 to 1732 +, or as One to the Root of Three. The Key-number of the series is found by abstracting from Three its own Root, thus (raising all values by 1000 to cover fractions, according to the usual method).

$$\frac{3000}{\text{minus } 1732} = 1268 = \text{E}\xi\ ου\ τα\ παντα.$$
Ἡ αληθοσυνη Θεου.
Ἡ ουσια ἡ μεγαλη Θεου.

This is the Building Number, that which geometrises (Γεωμετρει). It contains the potency of the double ΒΑΠΤΙΣΜΑ—634 + 634 = 1268.

From this we can proceed to build several series as follows—

The Key Applied.

$$1000$$
$$+\ 634$$

$$1634\ \text{Βαπτισμα Κυριου.} \quad \text{Αριθμος Βαπτισματος,}$$
$$+\ 634 \qquad \text{etc.}$$

$$2268\ \text{ΙΗΣΟΥΣ Ὁ ΑΝΘΡΩΠΟΣ.}$$
$$\text{ἡ ὁδος του πνευματος.}$$

The Annunciation

$$\text{ΜΑΡΙΑ} = 152 = \alpha\lambda\eta\theta\epsilon\iota\alpha\ \nu\iota\kappa\eta.$$
$$+\ \text{Αγγελος} = 312$$

reveal Ἡ Μητηρ $= 464$
$+$ Ἡ ἁγια Τριας $= 634$

Ἡ εκπορευσις $= 1098$ (The Procession of the
$= {}^{*}$Μαρια· το πνευμα.   Holy Ghost.)
$+$ Βαπτισμα $= 634$

Ἡ αρχη ζωης $= 1732$ ($\sqrt{3} \times 1000$)   Ὁ λυχνος
$+\ 634$ αγγελος.

ΙΗΣΟΥΣ Ὁ ΣΩΤΗΡ $= 2366$ $\dfrac{3+\sqrt{3}}{2} \times 1000$ Φως
†(φωνη εν ερημω)   Αδωναι.
$+$ ἁγιον ενδυμα $= 634$

Προβολη του φωτος $= 3000$ 3×1000 Λυχνος του υἱου.
$=$ Φως· ενδυμα κυριου.

---

* There is very early Christian authority for this in the 'Gospel according to the Hebrews' quoted by Origen and St. Jerome. See also 'Acts of St. Thomas'.

† Whence it will be seen that the φωνη εν ερημω is the germ of the threefold λογος, *plus* the power of Baptism, and that by the second operation of the same power the Trinity itself becomes manifest. It will be remembered in this connection that Ιωαννης stands for the triple LOGOS. Three is the number of the greatest and most profound of the Christian Mysteries—the Persons

or Ενδυμα ΑΔΩΝΑΙ } = 500
                   } + 866
                   ———
'Η Φωνη = 1366 $\dfrac{1+\sqrt{3}}{2} \times 1000$.
+ Βαπτισμα = 634
   ———
'Ο βοων εν ερημῳ = 2000   ενδυμα φως.

and Βαπτισμα = 634
  + ΑΔΩΝΑΙ = 866
    ———
  = ΦΩΣ = 1500 = $\dfrac{3}{2} \times 1000$.

Readers will easily discover other series for themselves. We have shewn the correspondences evoked by the addition of number to number, or by the converse method of subtraction, but from the nature of the series, which has to do with geometrical quantities, it will be found that processes of multiplication or division are wont to give similar results. Thus, for example, 1500, the number of Light, if divided by 634, gives us 2366, the digits of ΙΗΣΟΤΣ 'Ο ΣΩΤΗΡ, and if this be again divided by 634 the digits 3,732 are produced, in Gematria 373—the Logos, and representing the formula $2 + \sqrt{3}$.

It has been said of the Tenth Book of Euclid, which is the development of all the preceding ones, and deals with these 'irrational quantities', that it is "one of the most curious of Greek speculations. In this work Euclid

---

of the Godhead—and the aeonial mystery which the teaching of the Gematria presents is that which lies within and beyond this—the Generative principle in the Bosom of the Father. Our demonstration should serve to indicate how valuable the Gematria may be for the conservation of the purity of the text, and how great its corroborative value; and further than this, it will shew to what extent the original shade of meaning resident in such words as Βαπτισμα may have been lost in the mere idea of the rite, and how the spiritual conception may regain definiteness by the restoration of the key of the GNOSIS.

had evidently in mind the classification of incommensurable quantities: perhaps the circumference of the circle, which we know to have been an object of enquiry, was suspected of being incommensurable with its diameter, and hopes were perhaps entertained that a searching attempt to arrange the Incommensurables which ordinary geometry presents might enable the geometer to say finally to which, if any of them, the circle belongs. However this may be, Euclid investigates, by isolated methods, and in a manner which, *unless he has a concealed algebra*, is more astonishing than anything in the Elements, every possible variety of lines which can be represented by the formula

$$\sqrt{(\sqrt{a} \pm \sqrt{\beta})}$$

a and β representing two commensurable lines. He divides lines which can be represented by this formula into 25 species and he succeeds in detecting every possible species. He shews that every individual of every species in incommensurable with all the individuals of every other species; and also that no line of any species can belong to that species in two different ways, or for two different sets of values a and β."*

The Gematria appears to reflect this intention and to apply it to the description of the aeons and their formative principles as the intellectual counterpart of spiritual things. The wise men of old knew that the Mind of man was geometrical, being but a reflection of the Mind of God: but so little did the Church of the monastic ages care for geometry that Euclid came back to Europe through the Arabic!

---

* See Smith's Dictionary of Latin and Greek Biography, sub 'EUCLID' (italics ours).

The MYSTERION.

In Six days the Universe was created. Mystically, Six is the Formative principle of the Cosmos and Geometry gives her warrant to this.

In the Gematria this Sixfold nature is constantly expressed. In the ΑΠΟΡΡΟΙΑ 432 or 6 × 72, the name for that quality by which objects become visibly manifest; in the ΠΡΟΒΟΛΗ or Spatial projection which is 360, in the ΤΟΠΟΣ which is 720 or 6 × 120, and in the ΚΟΣΜΟΣ itself, whose number is 600, we find always this guiding principle. But the Parent, whose immanence in his work gives Life, is the One, and hence the Unity must be added to give the Numbers of Perfection. So 6, 12, 18, 24, 30, 36, 42, the first seven formative numbers, become by this addition 7, 13, 19, 25, 31, 37, and 43.

And the last, raised by the power of Ten, is the number of ΝΟΜΟΣ—the Law, and of Number itself—ΑΡΙΘΜΟΣ. And why this number is chosen for the purpose of symbolising the controlling factor is, on geometric grounds, quite clear, and capable of satisfactory proof, but all that can here be said is, that it controls, unites, and harmonises the measures of circles and rectilinear figures in a manner that no other simple number could do.

Now one of the Key Words in the Gnostic Gematria is ΜΥΣΤΗΡΙΟΝ, and ΤΟ ΜΥΣΤΗΡΙΟΝ is 1548, which is 36 × 43, implying the Law operating in all Creation. And this number is also the number of the Incommensurable Line, the ΓΡΑΜΜΗ ΑΣΥΜΜΕΤΡΟΣ which in its generic sense is the parent of Rational Form and Whole Things—the Manifestations of the Aeons.

And the first of these Incommensurables is the Root of TWO, represented by the digits 14142. The Voice of the Lord, the ΦΩΝΗ ΚΥΡΙΟΥ, sounds once and generates the number 2358 (these digits expressing an incommensurable quantity, rather nearer 2357). Twice it sounds and the number 4714 appears; a third time and the digits 7071 come to view, a fourth brings 9428 ($\frac{22}{7} \times 3000$), a fifth, and we have 1178·5, which is the number of ΜΥΣ-ΤΗΡΙΟΝ or α' Μυστηριον—1178 or 1179, both expressions being employed. A sixth time the Voice sounds, and there appears the perfect aeon 14142, or $\sqrt{2} \times 10,000$. The series may otherwise, and perhaps more fitly, be expressed as commencing with Unity, thus,

1, 2357, 4714, 7071, 9428, 11785, 14142.

The First Mystery is the Mystery of the ΑΛΦΑ—the Last or 24th Mystery is the Mystery of the ΩΜΕΓΑ. The 24 μυστηρια correspond to the 24 letters of the Greek Alphabet, with their three Ogdoads, or groups of Eight (in which Marcus the Gnostic traced the 888 of the Master). And 14142 divided by 24 gives the digits of the Penterema (589).

But when the Pistis Sophia tells us that the First Mystery is also the 24th mystery, a riddle offers itself for solution, and this riddle can only be solved by reference to the Geometry of the Α and the Ω.

The clue is supplied in the first instance by the reference in an early Christian hymn* to the Α and Ω in the similitude of the Triangle and the Square or Lozenge, to which forms these letters may easily be seen to approximate. The next clue is in the word ΩΜΕΓΑ itself which by Gematria is ΣΧΗΜΑ—a Form, the number being 849.

Now there is evidence in the Gematria that there are two ways in which a value may be expressed, namely, either in the ordinary way, or by its reciprocal, the number produced by its division into Unity.

---

* (Communicated.) It is regretted that at the moment of going to press this reference cannot be verified.

Thus when 849, the Omega, is divided into 1,000,000, the reciprocal is found to be 1178, the number of the first Mystery, the ΜΥΣΤΗΡΙΟΝ, so that the number of the first mystery is only the arithmetical counterpart of the number of the last, and the statement of the Pistis Sophia is to be comprehended in this sense.

But 1178 or 1179 are both expressions for geometrical values having reference to the Root of Two, and in particular are associated with that peculiarly Triangular solid, the Tetrahedron, for ·117859 is the Solidity of a Tetrahedron whose edge is 1·000 in length, and the volume of the corresponding cube is 1·000. But if the volume of the Tetrahedron is 1·000, then that of the Cube or Omega figure is to be expressed as 849 (i.e. 8·49).

The sixth term of the series, Φωνη Κυριου, is, as we have seen, 14142, expressive of the perfect aeon, and taking this as the sum of the mysteries of this (alphabetical) order, let us divide by 24, the number of the letters, and we obtain the digits 589, in Gematria the ΠΕΝΤΕΡΗΜΑ, the key-word of a certain passage in the Pistis Sophia, recovered by Dr. Lea. The passage in question runs as follows (Schwartze): 'Et inveni μυστηριον in meo ενδυματι scriptum in quique verbis (πεντερημα) quae pertinent ad altitudinem . . . .

Ζαμα ζαμα ωζζα ραχαμα ωζαι.

The number of the ΕΝΔΥΜΑ, in which this mystery is to be sought, is 500—one of the Lord's three robes of Light, which jointly make 1500 ΦΩΣ. Divide this 500 by the 11785 of the ΜΥΣΤΗΡΙΟΝ, and there appear the digits 4242 nearly. And 4242 is the sum, by Gematria, of the following:

Μυστηριον α' πεντερημα ζαμα ζαμα ωζζα ραχαμα ωζαι.

And 4242, divided by the number of the ΕΝΔΥΜΑ again gives the 849 of the Ωμεγα.

The Key Applied.

In such strange guise does this old Gnostic work give the kernel of the knowledge concerning these fundamental things of geometry. But the passage quoted goes on to say that the Zama, etc., has a solution. We give the whole of this passage in the words of Schwartze's translation.

'Factum igitur est, quum sol exortus esset in locis orientis, descendit magna δυναμις lucis, in qua meum ενδυμα, quod posui in vicesimo quarto μυστηριῳ, sicuti jam dixi vobis nunc. Et inveni μυστηριον in meo ενδυματι, scriptum in quinque verbis quae (pertinent) ad altitudinem : ζαμα ζαμα ωζζα ραχαμα ωζαι, cuius est solutio : μυστηριον, quod est extra in κοσμῳ (το εξωτερον εν κοσμῳ) cuius causa universum factum est, hoc est egressio omnis et elatio omnis,* hoc projecit emanationes omnes et haec, quae sunt in istis omnibus. Et huius causa μυστηριον quodquod factum est atque etiam eorum τοποι omnes. Veni ad nos, quod nos socia tua μελη. Nos autem (δε) omnes tecum quoque. Nos unus idemque atque (tu es) unus idemque (sc. tecum et nobiscum).

'Istud est primum μυστηριον quod factum est ab initio in hoc, qui ineffabilis, antequam προηλθε : atque nomen illius nos omnes sumus.'

Here is the statement clearly made—that the first mystery (1178·5) was made in that which is Ὁ ΑΡΡΗΤΟΣ (849)—the Ineffable—before it came forth. And who are the *We*?

Ἡ μονας εν τριαδι = 849 = Ἡ τριας εν μοναδι.
Ὁ τελειος ανηρ : = 849 = Ωμεγα.

Dr. Lea restores the Greek of Schwartze's translation 'in quinque verbis' as πεντερημα—here following on known models. If μυστηριον is the ρημα, the digits of the Πεντερημα should have some sort of correspondence. ΠΕΝΤΕΡΗΜΑ is by Gematria 589, and this sum, divided by ·5, produces 1178 = Μυστηριον. This seems good enough. Πεντερημα, then as 589 stands for the volume of an octahedron within the Tetrahedron which is the Μυστηριον, and is half the solidity of the latter.

But the Octahedron, whose edges are equal in measure

---

* The "egressio omnis et elatio omnis" might be restored as Ἡ Παναρχια and Ἡ Παντελεια—851 + 490—total 1341 = Ὁ Σταυρος—The Cross.

to those of the tetrahedron and the Cube of the Omega, has a volume four times greater than that of the Tetrahedron, and consequently 4·712 at this (the lesser) computation.

And 4712 is the Gematria value of the words
ΜΥΣΤΗΡΙΟΝ ΠΕΝΤΕΡΗΜΑ ΤΟ ΕΞΩΤΕΡΟΝ ΕΝ ΚΟΣΜΩ,
so that with this we have a series embracing Four related Solids, and representing the first three regular or platonic bodies, and each of their cubic contents or volumes is recorded with a precision quite extraordinary. There is first the innermost octahedron, the πεντερημα, next the tetrahedron containing it, which is the μυστηριον, then the outer octahedron, the μυστηριον πεντερημα το εξωτερον εν κοσμῳ, and finally the Cube, the Ωμεγα and last Mystery.*

The discovery of this series lays a secure foundation for the prosecution of further research and indicates in no uncertain manner the course that such research may now be permitted to take. What may be its destined influence in the sphere of theological studies it is not as yet easy to forecast, but the potentialities are vast and the fields opened to the view of scholars present an almost illimitable perspective.

1549.†

ΤΟ Α' ΜΥΣΤΗΡΙΟΝ.
THE FIRST MYSTERY.

(το α' ενταλμα πατρος—The First Precept of the Father.)

As an instance of the more obvious kind of Gematria to be found in the Coptic Gnostic books, the following is

---

* See Table, Appendix F.   † Representing $\frac{3\sqrt{3}+1}{4} \times 1000$.

The Key Applied.

given. On p. 13 of Schwartze's translation of the Pistis Sophia, par. 13, the second ΕΝΔΥΜΑ is spoken of in the following terms:—

"Et hoc ενδυμα . . . est in eo gloria nominis μυστηριον, μηνευτον, quod idem est primum preceptum, atque μυστηριον quinque χαραγμων, et μυστηριον magni πρεσβευτου huius, qui est ineffabilis, quod idem est magnum lumen. . . ."

The reader will note the peculiar spelling of πρεσβευτης for πρεσβυτης and of μηνευτης for μηνυτης.

The ενδυμα is one of the three great Robes of Light which are the vesture of the Lord, and are connected with the first mystery—that of the Alpha, which is the last mystery.*

Now ΤΟ Α' ΜΥΣΤΗΡΙΟΝ = 1549,
and the ΜΕΓΑ ΕΝΔΥΜΑ ΚΥΡΙΟΥ = 1549,
but this is also ΜΕΓΑ ΦΩΣ = 1549,
and, by the variation of the spelling,
ΜΕΓΑΣ ΠΡΕΣΒΕΥΤΗΣ = 1549.

So far, the coincidences are clearly of a nature which precludes any reasonable theory of chance, but this is not all. These ενδυματα are the robes of Jesus, and are of the nature of the Aeons, and the Aeon of Jesus is   ΑΙΩΝ ΙΗΣΟΥ = 1549.

The Gnostic books are also full of references to the ΧΩΡΗΜΑ, apparently a geometrical aeon, since it is found in connection with all the others, and   ΧΩΡΗΜΑ = 1549.

It is also the number of the πνευματικος λογος, and, in the Orphic mysteries, of the Founder of the Mysteries—ΤΕΛΕΤΑΡΧΗΣ = 1549.

---

* Readers may trace a connected symbolism in the Three Yellow Robes worn by the Buddhist priesthood.

And finally, as Light (φως μεγα), it is the number of the First Precept of the Omnipotent— ΤΟ Α' ΕΝΤΑΛΜΑ ΠΑΤΡΟΣ = 1549.

As evident in the βαπτισμα series and elsewhere unmistakeably in the Gematria, the Creative Logos of Light is indicated by the Root of Three.*

Regarding, then, the 1549 of this Mysterion as the arithmetical sign of this Power, let us look at its parent number.

Now as $\sqrt{3} : 3 :: 1549 : 2683$,
2683 is the parent Number, indicative of the Creator of Light, and we find this is, in Gematria, the value of the all-important

ΤΟ ΠΛΗΡΩΜΑ ΤΟΥ ΘΕΟΥ = 2683,
(The Pleroma, or Fulness, of God.)

and it is the number of the Creative Fiat 'Let there be Light!' for ΓΕΝΗΘΗΤΩ ΦΩΣ = 2683.

Light is in very truth the Aeon of all Power, and

ΑΙΩΝ ΠΑΝΤΟΚΡΑΤΩΡ = 2683,
(The Almighty Aeon.)

ΙΕΡΟΝ † ΤΟΥ ΣΩΤΗΡΟΣ = 2683,
ΑΛΦΑ· ΩΜΕΓΑ· Η ΕΚΚΛΗΣΙΑ ΚΥΡΙΟΥ = 2683,
Ο ΛΟΓΟΣ· Η ΑΡΧΗ ΤΗΣ ΖΩΗΣ = 2683.

These magnificent words, so grand, so simple and telling, all occurring on this individual number, bespeak some great principle to be looked for in the number itself, for no casual choice could have determined so grave a matter. And here we shall not be disappointed, for 2683 is again one of the numbers which is in perfect geometrical accord with those of Light and Baptism in the series we have given. For 2683 is one-half of 5366, and 5366 is 3 × 1500 plus 866—ΑΔΩΝΑΙ with a triple vesture of Light (ΦΩΣ

---

* Λογος φως = 1873 = Λογος κατα Μυστηριον — the title of the Book of ΙΕΟΥ or Η Εκκλησια του Α· Ω, and 1873·2 = (17 + $\sqrt{3}$) × 100.

† Or Η ΠΑΡΑΘΗΚΗ ΤΟΥ ΣΩΤΗΡΟΣ.

= 1500). And here Adonai and Jesus are one in the Gematria, for this is the Jesus Christ the Righteous of I. John ii. 2, who is the propitiation for the sins of the world,

$$\text{ΙΗΣΟΥΣ ΧΡΙΣΤΟΣ ΔΙΚΑΙΟΣ} = 2683.$$

The two related numbers are capable of a perfectly simple algebraical expression, and it may be well to shew this as an example of the law which governs the genuine Gematria for the definition of ideas concerning the Nature and Works of God.

To arrive at this we have to postulate the powers of the Number Ten as being figurative of the Ineffable Source of All, allowing that it may be a fitting symbol of that Ineffable, whilst carefully avoiding the common error of a superstitious attribution to the number itself, this being a symbol and a symbol only. Ten, in this connection, is the sum of the first four arithmetical powers, $1 + 2 + 3 + 4$, the Tetractys of the Pythagoreans.* These powers first exist as the simple Monad, Dyad, Triad, and Tetrad. Their Squares are the foundation of Form (viz. 1, 4, 9, and 16). Now $1 + 4 = 5$, and $1 + 9 = 10$, $16 - 1 = 15$, $16 + 4 = 20$, and $16 + 9 = 25$. In this lies the unique geometrical basis of the Denary system of Number which the sages of old gave to the world, and to which the world has found it necessary to adhere. But these whole-number powers are Static Powers, and the Active Powers or Logoi are in the roots of the Two and the Three, and the Creative Logos of Light is the Root of Three.

Hence the Gnostic conception of Deity as the Source of Light may be described mathematically in reference to this Gematria as

$$\frac{9 + \sqrt{3}}{4} \times 1000,$$ which is 2683—Το Πληρωμα του Θεου,

---

* Which appears in the Gnostic systems (*cf.* Irenaeus).

and His number may be further analysed into the following homogeneous parts,

(1) $\dfrac{3 + \sqrt{3}}{4} \times 1000 = 1183 = $ ΓΕΝΗΘΗΤΩ—Let there be!

(2) $\dfrac{3 + 3}{4} \times 1000 = 1500 = $ ΦΩΣ—Light!

$\overline{}$
2683

so that $\dfrac{3 + \sqrt{3}}{4} \times 1000$ is the Creative Principle,

and $\dfrac{3 + 3}{4} \times 1000$ is the First Creature—ΦΩΣ,

and the Creative Fiat—Το α' ενταλμα πατρος—has the number 1549, which is expressed algebraically as

$$\dfrac{9 + \sqrt{3}}{4 \times \sqrt{3}} \times 1000.$$

THE 153 FISHES AND THE UNBROKEN NET.

Perfect Symmetry of Form is typical of Regenerate and perfected Nature and the means whereby the geometrical perfections can be expressed in literary form is by the use of Number. But the numbers related to geometric form are mainly incommensurables, and for the purpose of the Gematria a whole-number convention has to be achieved, whereby each value shall be rationally represented and with approximate truth.

One of these integrating numbers is 153, the number of the Fishes in the unbroken net, in the miracle recorded in St. John xxi. This number was held by the Fathers to signify the Number of the Elect. And it is a very important example of the general method of the Gematria, since it stands for the harmonising of the Root, or Generative Power of THREE, with Unity. For the

The Key Applied.

benefit of readers who may be interested, we propose shortly to explain this 'mystery' on its mathematical side.

Numbers under 100 are easy to use in calculation and afford a convenient foundation for the building up of larger series by process of addition or multiplication. Hence some number or numbers less than 100 which might stand for this quantity would be a desideratum. There are three or more of such numbers, and three in particular which give a very close approximation to the truth—so close as abundantly to satisfy the purpose of the Gematria.

The first of these numbers is 26, which is the equivalent in Gematria of the Hebrew Tetragrammaton יהוה IHVH—Jehovah—or more properly Jahweh.

The second is 71, the foundation of the Greek Tetragram ΘΕΟΣ = God, which has the number 284, or 4 × 71.

The third and most perfect is formed by the union of the two foregoing. 26 + 71 = 97, and this is the foundation of the mystical Greek Tetragrammaton IEOY = 485 or 5 × 97.

26 is 15 × √3, 71 is 41 × √3, and 97 is 56 × √3, so that 15 : 26
41 : 71
56 : 97   whose sum = 153
are all expressive of the ratio 1 : √3.

All these numbers are the foundation of series having accordant meanings in the Gematria and by their union other concordances are framed. 97 + 56 is 153, and this is one of the principal numbers of this order. It symbolises Unity plus the generative power of the Three.

Eight being the number of the Saviour, and 153 that of the saved, the process of salvation is accomplished by the Net, which as TO ΔIKTYON has the number 8 × 153, or 1224, which number the fishes IXΘYEΣ (= 1224) may also claim. And it is the number of Ὁ ΠΑΤΡΙΚΟΣ ΛΟΓΟΣ—The Word of the Father. The Net of Salvation is also figured as the Walls of the Heavenly City, a four-square figure—ΤΑ ΤΕΙΧΗ—the Walls = 1224, and within the square lies the citadel, a circle of the same breadth whose measure is the measure of the New Jerusalem—Ἡ ΚΑΙΝΗ ἹΕΡΟΤΣΑΛΗΜ = 961, which is Heaven (ὁ οὐρανος).

The ΙΧΘΤΕΣ ρνγ΄ are thus 1377, equal to the Net and the 153, and this is the number in Gematria of the Α· Ω with the ΠΝΕΥΜΑ, and of the ΕΥΑΓΓΕΛΙΟΝ ΚΟΣΜΟΥ.

This rationalising of irrational quantities, and integrating of fractional numbers appears to be generally regarded in the Teaching of the Cabala as a type and symbol of Salvation. And the relation found to subsist between certain words, such as ΣΩΤΗΡ—Saviour, and ΙΧΘΤΣ—Fish, which is typical of a very numerous class, furnishes an excellent demonstration of the fact. The two words are found to have numbers related as $2 : \sqrt{3}$, or as the diameter of a circle to the side of an equilateral triangle within that circle. Reference to Euclid, Bk. I., prop. 1, will shew that the latter line lies within the

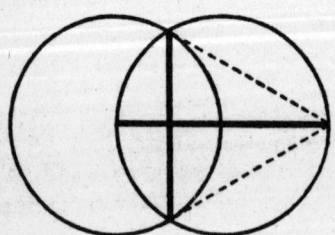

intersection of two equal circles, and is the measure of the 'Vesica' formed by their intersection. The historic and traditional importance of this Cabala, coupled with the extraordinary nature of the Gematria found to be connected with it, call for special mention.

CABALA OF THE FISH.

ΙΧΘΥΣ.
1219.
    Icthys, the Fish, is well-known as a frequent symbol of the Christian Faith, occurring in early inscriptions. As a natural type, it has an allegorical meaning, which may be rendered thus. The Fish, though living in the salt sea, is not penetrated by saltness. Even so, Jesus, incarnate in a world full of sin, is Himself free from sin, and His followers are also made free, those who are caught up in His net being saved from the salt waters.

The Gematria of the Icthys has survived in the Sibylline Acrostic, Ιησους Χρειστος Θεου 'Υιος Σωτηρ, the initials of which spell ΙΧΘΥΣ.

But in the orthodox Gematria it is now clearly seen to have a prominent place, aud its teaching is reinforced in the language of geometry and mathematical symbol. There can be no doubt that it is the same Mystery of the Icthys which is traditional in Sacred Art and Architecture, in the form of the Vesica Piscis. In this geometrical guise it is everywhere met with in ecclesiastical buildings of the mediaeval era, both as latent in the plan and proportions of Christian Temples, and apparent in the ornamental detail, where it is often associated with sculptured figures of Christ or of the Virgin.

The Vesica, as the diagram shews, is formed by the intersection of the arcs of two equal circles, and it contains a double equilateral triangle, AEBF, the figure of the Rhombus. The proportions of breadth to length, of Rhombus or Vesica, are as One to the Root of Three, and here we are again in the presence of the same geometrical teaching of the genesis of the Logos from the One, the Father, the Mystery of the Virgin Conception and Birth of the Logos of Truth.

The Vesica, by its measure of length, is the Ιχθυς

(1219 in Gematria), and the Diameter of the circle has a corresponding measure of 1408 = Σωτηρ—Saviour.

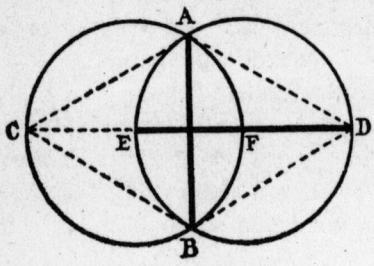

And 1408 : 1219, expresses with fair accuracy the ratio 2 : √3, since 1408 × ·866 = 1219·328. Either arm of the Cross formed by these two lines will thus be 609·66, integrated in Gematria as 610 = Ξυλον—The Cross.

These numbers give us the foundation of a whole geometric series whose Gematria is found to be no less harmonious. This we will now place before our readers. The first terms we find to be Παρθενος—The Virgin = 515, and the Virgin Conception—'Η καταβολη ἡ παρθενια = 704 —which is also the Conception of Truth—ἡ καταβολη αληθειας or the Higher Truth Itself—ἡ ουρανια αληθεια.

But 704 is half 1408—σωτηρ, and is thus the radius of the circle. And this is the geometrical Unit, and will figure in our series as 1.

Now   παρθενος   515
    + ἡ καταβολη αληθειας   704*

= 'Ο Λογος ἐκ πατρος 1219 which is Ιχθυς.

Hence we now have the first four terms of a mathematical series with an accordant teaching in Gematria, and a geometrical illustration, and these we may express as follows.

(1) 704 × 1.00 = 704   ἡ καταβολη αληθειας.
(2) 704 × 2.00 = 1408   ΣΩΤΗΡ—Saviour.
                        ΕΙΣ ΘΕΟΣ 'Ο ΜΟΝΟΣ ΚΑΙ
                        ΑΛΗΘΙΝΟΣ.

---

* Representing $\dfrac{10}{9+3\sqrt{3}} \times 1000$ (i.e. 704·4 etc.).

The Key Applied.

(3) $704 \times (\sqrt{3} - 1) = 515$ ΠΑΡΘΕΝΟΣ—The Virgin.

(4) $704 \times \sqrt{3} = 1219$ ΙΧΘΥΣ, also
Ο ΛΟΓΟΣ ΕΚ ΠΑΤΡΟΣ.
Καταβασις Θεου.
Ἑρμηνεια κυριου.
(ἡ γυνη 469 + ὁ ὑιος 750 = 1219 = παρθενος + ἡ καταβολη αληθειας.)

And from these we may proceed to develop:

(5) $704 \times \dfrac{\sqrt{3}}{2} = 610$ Ξυλον—The Cross. { Arm of Cross.

(6) $704 \times \dfrac{1}{2} = 352$ Ἡ ὁδος—The Way. { Type of Christ.

(7) $704 \times (\sqrt{3}+1) = 1923$ ΧΡΙΣΤΟΣ Ο ΛΟΓΟΣ.
This is the figure of the Cross in the Vesica, the union of the 1219 and 704.

But the following must be noted:

(a) $\underset{\text{παρθενος}}{515} + \underset{\text{σωτηρ}}{1408} = 1923$ Χριστος ὁ λογος.

(b) $\underset{\substack{\text{ὁ Θεος}\\\text{πατηρ}}}{843} + \underset{\substack{\text{το πνευμα}\\\text{ἁγιον}}}{1080} = 1923$ (God the Father, and the Holy Spirit, from whom proceed Christ the Word.)

And the 1923, as the union of the One with the Power of Three, symbolised by the two geometric measures, has exactly the same intention as the 153 of the Miraculous Draught—as we have already shewn. For that number stands for the same mathematical relation, viz. 97 : 56. And on the larger scale of the Icthys Gematria we find that the Lord's Draught of Fishes is

ρνγ' του Κυριου = 1923,

and the figures of the Fish and of Baptism give us again the number of the Logos, for

$$\begin{aligned}\text{Ὁ Ἰχθυς} \quad & 1289 \\ \text{Βαπτισμα} \quad & \underline{634} \\ = \ & 1923.\end{aligned}$$

We can now go further with our series. The next term is the measure of the whole cross, AB + ED.

(8) AB+ED
$= 2 + \sqrt{3} \times 704 = 2627$ Ὁ ΑΡΙΘΜΟΣ ΤΗΣ ΣΩΤΗΡΙΑΣ.
ΕΝΔΥΜΑ ΤΗΣ ΣΩΤΗΡΙΑΣ.
Λογος του Θεου Κυριου.
Ὁ Λογος εκ πατρος· σωτηρ.
Μεγας λογος του Θεου πατρος.

(9) AEF (triangle) or CEFD (Length of the greater Rhombus)
$= 704 \times 3.00 = 2112$ ΑΠΟΡΡΟΙΑ ΧΡΙΣΤΟΥ.
Ιησους το Δικτυον (Jesus, the Net).
Το δικτυον εστι λογος.
Μεγας ιχθυς Εμμανουηλ.

The greater rhombus is the type of the Net—Το δικτυον—containing the Vesica of the Icthys.

(10) AEBF (Rhombus)
$= 704 \times 4.00 = 2816$ ΙΗΣΟΥΣ Ὁ ΧΡΙΣΤΟΣ ΑΛΗΘΙΝΟΣ.

(11) AEBF (Vesica)
$= 704 \times \dfrac{4\pi}{3} = 2950$ Ὁ ΑΡΙΘΜΟΣ ΤΟΥ ΧΡΙΣΤΟΥ.
Ενδυμα του Χριστου.
Ἡ τραπεζα του σωτηρος.
Ἡ γεωμετρια σωτηρος.

The Key Applied.

(12) The Spherical Triangle on AEF, which has the same measure as the semicircle on ED or as a circle of which EF is the diameter, is one of the most important of the series and is expressed thus:—

AEF (Spherical)
$= 704 \times \pi = 2213$ Ὁ ΛΟΓΟΣ ΤΟΤ ΚΥΡΙΟΤ
(The Word of the Lord).

N.B. $704 \times \dfrac{22}{7} = 2212.57$.

(13) As 1219 is the length of the Vesica, it is also that of the base of the equilateral triangle ABD. Two sides of this triangle are raised upon the third, which is Ὁ λογος εκ πατρος, and the value of the two is thus expressed:—

AD + BD
$= 704 \times 2\sqrt{3} = 2438$ ΙΗΣΟΤΣ Ὁ ΧΡΙΣΤΟΣ.

(14) All three sides:—
AB + AD + BD
$= 704 \times 3\sqrt{3} = 3657$ ΙΗΣΟΤΣ ΧΡΙΣΤΟΣ Ὁ ΙΧ-
ΘΤΣ.
ΙΙΣΟΤΣ Ὁ ΧΡΙΣΤΟΣ· Ὁ
ΛΟΓΟΣ ΕΚ ΠΑΤΡΟΣ.

All the foregoing are linear measures, but those of area appear equally to give interesting results.

(a) Area of Triangle on base, 704.

$704^2 \times \dfrac{\sqrt{3}}{4} = 2146$ etc.   ΙΗΣΟΤΣ Ὁ ΛΕΙΤΟΤΡΓΟΣ.

(b) Area of Rhombus or Double Triangle, expressed as 4291-2.

$4291 =$ ΙΗΣΟΤΣ ΧΡΙΣΤΟΣ ΕΣΤΙ ΣΩΤΗΡ.
$4292 =$ ΧΡΙΣΤΟΣ ΥΙΟΣ ΤΟΤ ΠΑΝΤΟΚΡΑΤΟΡΟΣ.

(c) Area of the Spherical Triangle, by convention
$$= 3946 = \text{ΙΗΣΟΥΣ ΧΡΙΣΤΟΣ Ό ΥΙΟΣ ΑΛΗΘΙΝΟΣ}.$$

(d) Area of the Triangle ABD. This is most nearly expressed in hundreds by the digits 644, which is the number of Emmanuel.
$$644 = \text{ΕΜΜΑΝΟΥΗΛ}.$$

(e) Area of the greater Rhombus, 1288, or, by another convention, 1289.
$$1288 = \text{Ἡ ΘΕΟΤΗΣ ΙΗΣΟΥ} \text{ (The Divinity of Jesus)}.$$
$$1289 = \text{Ό ΙΧΘΥΣ}—\text{The Fish}.$$

We have set out this series in some detail, since there is a cumulative value which tends to strengthen the proof. But what has been shewn does not exhaust the possibilities of this amazing Cabala. It is clear however that the symbol refers not only to the Christian Faith and to its Members, but, by this body of geometrical teaching, to its Founder as well, as the Word of Truth proceeding from the Father and through the Spirit.

Thus in the secret communications of the early Christians the Sign of the Fish is used as a token of brotherhood and as a credential.

And its number is that of the Author and Finisher of the Faith—Ό ΛΟΓΟΣ ΕΚ ΠΑΤΡΟΣ and ΤΟ ΩΜΕΓΑ.

At the close of what may be termed the first great encyclical letter to the Gentile converts and to all whom it might concern, which we have in Acts xv., appears the word ΕΡΡΩΣΘΕ—Farewell. This word, behind its simple and obvious significance, would hide a further meaning which might quite readily carry with it the testimony to the authenticity of the letter, for the number of ΕΡΡΩΣΘΕ is 1219—the Sign of the Fish and of the Saviour—Ό ΛΟΓΟΣ ΕΚ ΠΑΤΡΟΣ.

We must now take leave of our readers. Enough, we trust, has been said to make clear the purport and the trend of what has been discovered. The triple chain of correspondences, first, the harmony of number and meaning in groups of words on individual numbers; second, the harmonic sequences of numbers built upon the Roots which are the Formative Principles in Nature; and third, the answering sequences of meaning in the Gematria which appear so consistently to explain and elucidate the doctrines of the Church, proclaim the fact that here we have before our eyes the operation of Law, not Chance, and that no casual or superstitious fancy, but a high degree of Knowledge and Intelligence, laid within the Sacred Books this unseen foundation.

But we do not miss the real significance of that which this teaching implies. When we contemplate the Symmetric Forms with which it deals, forms composite yet moulding their many parts into perfect wholes, everywhere the Great Law holds, the Law of the perfect union of the Lesser *in* the Greater, and of the Greater *with* the Lesser forms which are the perfect miniatures of the Greater. So we see the great Figure of the Church, which is the congregation of units whose being is patterned on the Universal Truth, mirrored as fidelity to her Form, and thus sharing the eternal or aeonial Life of the great Exemplar.

As Stones of the living Temple each one fits and fills his niche, and the Temple is not perfect until All the Stones are in their appointed place and the Lord has made up His jewels. In coming face to face with the reality of this teaching the disciple loses sight of his fancied isolation and knows that he is One with his Master and with all his Fellows, and that all are members one of another, since each is necessary to the whole. And with this truth it may be that the future of Religion among the nations of the Earth is bound up.

THE DIGAMMA.

Ϝ, The Διγαμμα. An obsolete letter corresponding to the Hebrew Vav, and in sound like a W. Retained as a numerical sign, it became gradually simplified in form until it was no more than a large comma, the επισημον or στιγμα. The place of the Digamma is taken in the Roman Alphabet by the F. In the Greek Alphabet, as reconstructed, the Digamma disappears as a letter, but a labial φ (ph) is introduced. There is no proved connection between the two, but a coincidence must be noticed. Φ has the numeral value 500, which is that of Σ and T combined, since Σ = 200 and T = 300. Both Σ and T retain their individual values in the Gematria, but where they occur together they make a semi-compound letter, and this, in later Greek, is recognised as a compound letter 'stau', with a sign 'ς' so like the στιγμα as to be for all practical purposes identical. And in mediaeval Greek they are clearly one.

Now for the purposes of Gematria the letters most frequently employed are necessarily those which denote the unit values. For example, the word αληθεια—Truth—is composed chiefly of such numbers, being $1+30+8+9+5+10+1 = 64$, and the number 6 would be one whose exclusion would be most inconvenient. Consequently it would be quite reasonable to assume that endeavours would be made to retain this value.

The fusion of the two signs, the στιγμα with the compound σταυ, might readily suggest an underlying element of intention. As to this there seems no direct evidence. But on the other hand there is in the Gematria itself some very suggestive internal evidence pointing to such a use, and a typical example of the Gematria so obtained is the word σταυρος—The Cross—which, by counting σ.τ. as 6, gives the number 777—a highly symbolic one in connection with the 888 of Jesus.

And the value 500 being supplied by φ, there would no longer be the same urgency for this numeration in all cases where the σ.τ. are employed. Hence on general grounds we have included σταυρος in the list of 37 multiples (Appendix C).

APPENDIX A.

485 = IEOY, identical by Gematria with IOYΔA and with IEΣOΣ—the latter said to be the original spelling of the name of Jesus in Pilate's inscription in the Church of Sta. Croce at Rome. Ὁ Παναγιος has the same number. The Tetragrammaton IAOU cited by Clem. Al. is another form of this, having the number 481 which is 37×13 the Jewish sacred number. The Jewish cabalists were accustomed to substitute for the Divine Name the word באב־שלום BAB-SHaLOM = Gate of Salem or Peace (ειρηνης = 381), with the number 381, which is the measure of the circle contained in the square of 485 perimeter, and by Gematria the ραμπλιον of the Persian astronomers.

Αδωναι—866—is $485 + 381$.

485 is notable for the following peculiar powers as a number in the geometrical series and as integrating the roots of 2, 3, and 6.

(1) 485 = The cube of Seven $\times \sqrt{2}$ (343×1.4144).
    = Four times 70 $\times \sqrt{3}$ (280×1.7321).
    = Nine times 22 $\times \sqrt{6}$ (198×2.4495).
       The last is particularly exact.

(2) 485 = Doubly a Square of the Hypothenuse, since
       $22^2 + 1 = 485$
    and $17^2 + 14^2 = 485$.

As the 29th of the series of Hypothenuse squares which are capable of being resolved into two or more pairs of Squares it appears important. There are in the Books of IEOU twenty-eight surviving diagrams of concentric squares of IEOU, with indications of a twenty-ninth, a leaf being lost. There seems ground for supposing that these diagrams may have reference to the system of hypothenuse squares, and the fundamental importance attributed by the old geometers to these squares is well-known and can be readily understood by reference to the early editions of Euclid. They have various geometric uses.

(3) $485 = 20^2 + 9^2 + 2^2$. $16^2 + 15^2 + 2^2$.
$\qquad 20^2 + 7^2 + 6^2$. $15^2 + 14^2 + 8^2$.

(4) $\sqrt[3]{485} = \dfrac{\pi \times 10}{4}$ nearly $(= 7.857) = 10 \times \frac{11}{14}$, which is precisely the old convention. Note that $7857 = 97 \times 81$ or $(2^4 + 3^4) \times 3^4$.

(5) $485 = (3 + 2) \times (3^4 + 2^4)$.

APPENDIX B.

Of the Square and Circle contained.

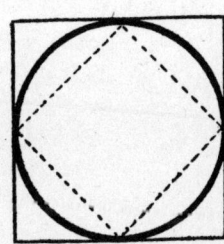

(1) When the perimeter of the Square is 1270, that of the circle is 998, and

1270 = Νυμφιος—The Bridegroom.

998 = Νυμφη—The Bride, the 'Κορη κοσμου' of certain Gnostics.

―――

2268 = Ιησους ὁ ανθρωπος.

(2) When the Square is 656, the circle is 515, and the square lozenge within the square is 464.

656 = Μεσσιας—The Messiah.
515 = Παρθενος—The Virgin.
464 = Ἡ Μητηρ—The Mother.

464 + 515 is the Γυνη ἡλιου as well as Ἡ παρθενος μητηρ.

656 + 515 is 1171, the number of the Πανσοφος, the second Profundity of the Gnostic aeons.

656 + 464 is 1120, which is the Τριδυναμεις of the Coptic books, and of the Gnostic system generally.

656 is 464 + 192 = Ἡ μητηρ Μαριαμ.

(3) When the Square is 1224—the circle is 961 (or 31^2). These, as already shewn, are τα τειχη and Ἡ καινη Ἱερουσαλημ—the Heavenly city and its peribolus. But the joint number 1224 + 961 is the Τειχος Κυριου—2185, and the lozenge within the square measures 866—Αδωναι.

(4) If the measure of the square be 2185, the circle becomes 1716—1717, and the inner square or lozenge 1545.

2185 = ‘Ο αιων του Θεου (τειχος κυριου).

1545 = ‘Ο Τεκτων—The Builder—title of Christ.

And 2185 − 1545 = 640 = The Kingdom of Peace, which is βασιλεια ειρηνης.

The circle, taken at the lesser valuation 1716, stands for ἡ ψυχη = The Soul.

APPENDIX C.

NAMES, EPITHETS, AND TYPES of CHRIST, APPEARING IN THE GEMATRIA OF THE SACRED BOOKS AS MULTIPLES OF 37, TOGETHER WITH OTHER EXAMPLES.

PRELIMINARY NOTE BY DR. LEA.

This list, apart from its intrinsic interest, is a sample of the method adopted in the investigation. A careful index is being compiled by Mr. Bond of all words and phrases which seem likely to have been constructed or selected to convey meanings apart from their ordinary literary sense.

Coincidences purely accidental must necessarily occur, and something like three per cent. of all words and phrases will be multiples of Thirty-seven by the mere operation of the doctrine of Chance.

But when a large collection exhibits peculiarities for which the doctrine of Chance cannot wholly account, then other causes must be looked for and will probably be discovered. This method has been successfully applied in other branches of science, and, though very slow, is extremely effective.

T. S. L.

37		ABEL (Heb.) הבל.	
185	37×5	Ὁ ῬΑΒΒΙ = The Master.	
259	37×7	ΒΑΣΙΛΕΙΑ = Kingdom.	
333	37×9	Ἡ ἘΛΠΙΣ = Hope.	

407   37 × 11   Ἡ ΚΛΗΡΟΝΟΜΙΑ = The Inheritance. Isa. lviii. 14.

(ἡ κληρονομια ἁγιων = 1271
= ἡ γνωσις and σταυρος).

481   37 × 13   Ἡ ΓΕΝΕΣΙΣ—The Beginning.

Ἡ ΕΠΙΣΚΟΠΗ, I. Pet. ii. 12 = The Lord's Visitation.

ΕΠΙΣΚΟΠΕΙΑ = Overseership.

This is the number of the Tetragrammaton ΙΑΟΥ mentioned by Clement of Alexandria: also of the ecclesiastical formula Π·Υ·Α meaning the Three Persons—Πατηρ, Ὑιος, and Ἁγιον πνευμα. 481 is the measure of the circle whose diameter is the 153 of the Elect.

518   37 × 14   Ἡ ΘΥΡΑ—The Door. Epithet of Christ. S. John x. 9.

ΠΥΛΗ—The Gate. Matt. vii. 13, 14.

ΟΙ ΚΛΗΤΟΙ—The Elect.

555   37 × 15   ΕΠΙΘΥΜΙΑ. The Desire of Jesus to eat the Passover in fellowship. S. Luke xxii. 15.

592   37 × 16   ΘΕΟΤΗΣ — Godhead; also ἉΓΙΟΤΗΣ, ΑΓΑΘΟΤΗΣ.

This is the number of the Interpreter Εξηγητης, and of the Ρητολογια or framing of sentences; a term also employed by geometers to imply 'the logic of "rational" lines'. It enters into Aegypto-Greek Gematria as the number of ΣΑΡΑΠΙΣ and of ΑΜΥΝ-ΡΑ.

666   37 × 18   Not emblematic of Christ in our Scriptures but originally appertaining to the Solar Divinity in the Greek Ὁ ΣΕΡΑΠΙΣ and ΤΕΙΤΑΝ, in the Hebrew סורת (Sorath), שמש־יהוה SheMeSh-IaHVeH — the Sun of Jahweh, שלוש ShiLLVSh (the

dotted ל is counted double) — the Rabbinical name for the Triune God.

703 37 × 19 Ὁ ΘΕΟΣ ΙΣΡΑΗΛ. ΘΕΟΣ ΔΑΥΙΔ. Ὁ ἉΓΙΟΣ ΙΣΡΑΗΛ. ΧΑΝΑΑΝ (The Promised Land).

740 37 × 20 Not a number of Christ, but, like 666, a cosmic number, being that of the ΚΥΚΛΟΣ —or Cycle, of ΚΤΙΣΙΣ—Creation; the יכין IaKIN of the Hebrew temple symbolism, the solar ΑΙΔΟΝΕΥΣ of Aegypto-Greek worship, Ἡ ΘΕΡΜΟΤΗΣ—Heat, ΑΙΘΕΡΟΣ ΜΕΛΟΣ—The Music of the Spheres, and the Ὁ ΕΠΙ ΠΑΣΙ ΘΕΟΣ of the Platonists.

777 37 × 21 Traditionally the number of ΣΤΑΥΡΟΣ—the Cross, spelt with the Digamma for σ.τ. (= 6), see note at end of text.

851 37 × 23 ὙΠΑΡΞΙΣ — Substance. Epithet of Christ. See Heb. x. 34.

888 37 × 24 ΙΗΣΟΥΣ. ΛΟΓΟΣ ΕΣΤΙ. Ἡ ΖΩΗ ΕΙΜΙ.

999 37 × 27 ἹΕΡΕΥΣ ΣΑΛΗΜ.
TO ἈΡΡΗΤΟΝ—The Ineffable.
ΕΙΣ ΘΕΟΣ Ὁ ΜΟΝΟΣ (Creeds).

1036 37 × 28 Ἡ ΑΝΑΣΤΑΣΙΣ ΕΙΜΙ, 'I am the Resurrection', words of Christ.

1073 37 × 29 Ὁ ΘΕΟΣ ΤΗΣ ΓΗΣ. Genesis xxiv. 3.

1110 37 × 30 ΣΑΒΒΑΤΟΝ ΘΕΟΥ.
TO ἉΓΙΑΣΜΑ ΘΕΟΥ.
ΤΑ ΠΑΝΤΑ ΚΑΙ ΕΝ ΠΑΣΙ (Χριστος). Coloss. iii. 11.
Again a cosmic number, being that of Ὁ ΜΙΚΡΟΣ ΚΟΣΜΟΣ, and Ὁ ΚΟΣΜΟΣ Ὁ ὍΛΟΣ.

1184 37 × 32 Ὁ ΘΕΟΣ ΚΟΣΜΟΠΟΙΟΣ.

1221 37 × 33 ΘΑΥΜΑΣΤΟΣ = wonderful. Epithet of the Messiah. Isaiah ix. 6.

Investigation of the Cabala.

1258 37 × 34 Ὁ ΛΕΙΤΟΥΡΓΟΣ—The Minister. Epithet of Christ. Heb. viii. 2.

1332 37 × 36 ΑΛΦΑ· Ω. Cosmic and Solar. The number of the ΧΝΟΥΒΙΣ of the Gnostic Inscriptions.

1369 37 × 37 The Square of 37. ΕΙΣ ΘΕΟΣ Ὁ ΚΥΡΙΟΣ, Ὁ ΘΕΟΣ ΖΩΗΣ and the ΕΙΚΩΝ ΘΕΟΥ, etc.

1443 37 × 39 Ὁ ΛΟΓΟΣ ΚΥΡΙΟΥ.
Ἡ ΕΙΡΗΝΗ ΤΟΥ ΘΕΟΥ.
(Ἐμμανουηλ ἐστι θεος.)

1480 37 × 40 ΧΡΙΣΤΟΣ.
ΥΙΟΣ ΚΥΡΙΟΣ.
Ὁ ΚΥΡΙΟΣ· Ὁ ΔΙΔΑΣΚΑΛΟΣ.
Ἡ ΘΕΟΤΗΣ ΥΙΟΥ.
ΙΗΣΟΥΣ ΘΕΟΤΗΣ.
Ἡ ἉΓΙΩΣΥΝΗ.
Ἡ ΤΡΑΠΕΖΑ ΜΥΣΤΙΚΗ (The Early Christian Altar).
ΧΝΟΥΜΙΣ. P. I. (Gnostic gems.)

1517 37 × 41 ΔΥΝΑΜΙΣ ΚΑΙ ΣΟΦΙΑ, *cf.* I. Cor. i. 24.
Ἡ ΑΡΧΗ ΚΟΣΜΟΥ.

1554 37 × 42 ΑΝΑΣΤΑΣΙΣ ΣΑΡΚΟΣ.
ΜΕΣΣΙΑΣ ἩΜΩΝ.

1591 37 × 43 ΑΙΩΝΟΤΟΚΟΣ—Parent of the Eternal, or of the Aeon. Synesius 322a.
ΠΝΕΥΜΑ ΖΩΗΣ.

1628 37 × 44 ΚΕΦΑΛΗ ΓΩΝΙΑΣ — Head of the Corner. Epithet of Christ. Matt. xxi. 42.
Ἡ ΠΙΣΤΙΣ ΚΑΙ Ἡ ΣΟΦΙΑ.

1665 37 × 45 ΑΛΦΑ ΩΜΕΓΑ· ΘΕΩΣ.
ΑΡΙΘΜΟΣ ΘΕΟΥ ΠΑΤΡΟΣ.

1739 37 × 47 Ὁ ΚΥΡΙΟΣ ΒΟΗΘΟΣ ΜΟΥ. Psalms.

1776 37 × 48 Ἡ ΣΩΤΗΡΙΑ ΙΣΡΑΗΛ. Ἡ Σωτηρια is a frequent type of Christ in the New Testament Books.

Appendix. 69

ΙΗΣΟΥΣ ΕΣΤΙ ΛΟΓΟΣ.
ΤΟ ΑΛΗΘΙΝΟΝ ΜΥΣΤΗΡΙΟΝ.
ΚΑΤΕΧΩΝ. A word whose real meaning has been the subject of much speculation (see Döllinger's *First Age of the Church*, Appendix.)

1813 37 × 49 ΚΥΡΙΟΣ ΣΑΒΑΩΘ—Lord of Hosts. Isa. ix. 7.
(Εμμανουηλ ὁ υιος Δαυιδ.)
(Ὁ υιος Δαυιδ κατα σαρκα.)

1850 37 × 50 This is the number of the ΧΩΡΗΜΑΤΑ of the Gnostic books: also of the Αρχη αιωνιος; Ἡ φωνη θεου; Ὁ Γεωμετρης ὁ μεγας; Ἡ επιγνωσις θεου, and the Ὁ Μεγας Προπατωρ of the Book of Ιεου. Clearly a number of the Cosmogony.

1887 37 × 51 ΣΩΤΗΡΙΟΝ ΙΣΡΑΗΛ. Epithet of Christ. See 2257. (*cf.* Ps. xiv. 7 and liii. 6.)
ΤΟ ΓΕΝΟΣ ΤΟΥ ΔΑΥΙΔ.

1924 37 × 52 Ὁ ΘΕΟΣ ΤΟΥ ΚΟΣΜΟΥ.
Ὁ ΚΟΣΜΟΣ ΤΟΥ ΘΕΟΥ.

1961 37 × 53 ΑΡΧΗ ΤΟΥ ΒΙΟΥ.
ΧΡΙΣΤΟΣ Ἡ ΓΕΝΕΣΙΣ.
Ὁ ουρανος κυριου.

1998 37 × 54 ΝΥΜΦΗ ΚΥΡΙΟΥ.
Ἡ ΠΑΣΑ ΨΥΧΗ. *cf.* Ep. Rom. xiii. 1.
ἉΓΙΟΝ ἉΓΙΩΝ ΚΥΡΙΟΥ.
ΠΟΙΗΤΗΣ ΑΟΡΑΤΩΝ (Creeds).
Ἡ ΑΡΧΗ ΠΑΝΤΩΝ.
Ὁ ΥΙΟΣ ΕΚ ΤΗΣ ΠΑΡΘΕΝΟΥ (Creeds).
Ὁ ΧΡΙΣΤΟΣ Ὁ ΑΛΗΘΙΝΟΣ.

2035 37 × 55 ΤΕΙΧΟΣ ΠΥΡΟΣ — Wall of Fire. Type of Christ. Zech. ii. 5.
Ὁ ΠΑΤΗΡ ΕΝ ΟΥΡΑΝΩ.
ΓΝΩΣΙΣ ΤΗΣ ΑΛΗΘΕΙΑΣ.
ΣΟΦΙΑ ΤΟΥ ΘΕΟΥ.

2072 37 × 56   ΤΟ ΑΛΦΑ, ΤΟ Ω.
               Ἡ ΓΝΩΣΙΣ Α.Ω.
               Ἡ ΕΚΚΛΗΣΙΑ ΤΟΥ ΚΥΡΙΟΥ.
               Ἡ ΓΕΩΜΕΤΡΙΑ ΚΟΣΜΟΥ.
               ΓΕΩΜΕΤΡΙΚΗ ΣΟΦΙΑ.
               Ἡ ΕΝΘΟΥΣΙΑΣΤΙΚΗ ΣΟΦΙΑ.   (= Divination.)

2109 37 × 57   ΥΙΟΣ ΔΑΒΙΔ· ΣΩΤΗΡ.
               ΣΩΤΗΡ ΠΑΝΤΟΣ.
               ΦΩΝΗ ΠΑΤΡΟΣ.
               Ὁ ΕΝΣΩΜΑΤΟΣ ΛΟΓΟΣ.
               ΑΡΧΗ ΤΟΥ ΝΟΜΟΥ.

2146 37 × 58   ΑΛΙΕΙΣ ΑΝΘΡΩΠΩΝ—Fishers of Men. Matt.
               iv. 19. Mark i. 17.
               ΟΙ ΑΙΩΝΕΣ ΚΥΡΙΟΥ.

2183 37 × 59   ΚΕΦΑΛΗ ΥΠΕΡ ΠΑΝΤΑ ΤΗ ΕΚΚΛΗΣΙΑ—Head
               over all to the Church. Epithet of
               Christ. Ep. Eph. i. 22.

2220 37 × 60   A cosmic and Solar number.
               ΕΓΩ ΑΛΦΑ ΚΑΙ ΩΜΕΓΑ.
               Ἡ ΥΠΟΣΤΑΣΙΣ ΠΑΤΡΟΣ.
               The name ΧΡΙΣΤΟΦΟΡΟΣ, by which members
               of the primitive church were designated,
               has this number.
               ΤΟ ΟΝΟΜΑ ΣΩΤΗΡΙΑΣ.

2257 37 × 61   ΤΟ ΣΩΤΗΡΙΟΝ ΙΣΡΑΗΛ. *cf.* Ps. xiv. 7 and
               liii. 6. (Το σωτηριον του Ἰσραηλ.)
               ΚΙΒΩΤΟΣ ΝΩΕ—Noah's Ark.

2294 37 × 62   ΠΡΩΤΟΤΟΚΟΣ ΘΕΟΣ. *cf.* Heb. i. 6.
               ΠΛΗΡΩΜΑ ΘΕΟΥ ΠΑΤΡΟΣ. (See also 2664.)

2331 37 × 63   ΙΗΣΟΥΣ Ὁ ΛΟΓΟΣ ΚΥΡΙΟΥ.
               'ΕΓΩ ΕΙΜΙ'· Ὁ ΛΟΓΟΣ ΖΩΗΣ.
               Ὁ ΚΥΡΙΟΣ ΓΕΩΜΕΤΡΗΣ.
               Ὁ ΓΕΩΜΕΤΡΗΣ ΚΟΣΜΟΥ.
               Ἡ Ἀορατος + Πιστις Σοφια.

Appendix. 71

2368 37 × 64 ΙΗΣΟΥΣ ΧΡΙΣΤΟΣ.
Ὁ ΘΕΟΣ ΤΩΝ ΘΕΩΝ—Ὁ ἍΓΙΟΣ ΤΩΝ ἉΓΙΩΝ.
ΤΟ ἍΓΙΟΝ ἉΓΙΩΝ ΚΥΡΙΟΥ.

2442 37 × 66 ΙΗΣΟΥΣ ΜΕΣΣΙΑΣ ἩΜΩΝ.

2479 37 × 67 Ὁ λογος εστι του πατρος.
Χριστος εστι θεου.

2516 37 × 68 ΧΑΡΑΓΜΑ ΤΟΥ ΚΥΡΙΟΥ.
ΤΟ ΠΝΕΥΜΑ ΤΟΥ ΚΟΣΜΟΥ.
Ἡ ΨΥΧΗ ΚΟΣΜΟΥ.
A Gnostic number on which we find χωρα ζωης (Book of Ieou. Schmidt, p. 306), φυλακες πυλων (do., p. 207).

2590 37 × 70 ΤΑ ΠΑΝΤΑ ΚΑΙ ΕΝ ΠΑΣΙ ΧΡΙΣΤΟΣ.
The number of the Τοπος φωτος of the Books of IEOU, and of the Δωρεα Χριστου = Baptism of the Early Church.

2627 37 × 71 ΙΧΘΥΣ ΣΩΤΗΡ.
ΕΝΔΥΜΑ ΤΗΣ ΣΩΤΗΡΙΑΣ.
(Καταπετασμα Σωτηρος.)
Ὁ ΤΗΣ ΣΩΤΗΡΙΑΣ ΑΡΙΘΜΟΣ.
ΣΩΤΗΡ ΚΑΙ ΛΕΙΤΟΥΡΓΟΣ.
ΤΟ ΕΥΑΓΓΕΛΙΟΝ ΧΡΙΣΤΟΥ.
The peculiar geometric and doctrinal importance of this number is explained in the text (p. —) where a diagram is given, shewing the connection of the ιχθυς, σωτηρ and ξυλον lines. The number 2627 has also cosmic analogies, and is, by Gematria, that of the Zodiacal Circle Ὁ ζωοφορος κυκλος, and of Ὁ ουρανος εν σφαιρῳ (σφαιρος in Empedocles).
As the 71st multiple of 37 it is doubly a number of God (Θεος being 4 × 71) and hence we find it gives us
ΛΟΓΟΣ ΤΟΥ ΘΕΟΥ ΚΥΡΙΟΥ = 2627 = ΙΧΘΥΣ ΣΩΤΗΡ, etc.

2664	37 × 72	ΤΟ ΠΛΗΡΩΜΑ ΘΕΟΥ ΠΑΤΡΟΣ.
2701	37 × 73	Ὁ ΑΙΩΝ ΤΟΥ ΚΥΡΙΟΥ.

Also the number of Αποστολος Χριστου.

2738	37 × 74	ΕΙΣ ΘΕΟΣ Ὁ ΠΑΤΗΡ ΧΡΙΣΤΟΥ.
		ΒΑΣΙΛΕΥΣ ΑΝΘΡΩΠΩΝ.
2775	37 × 75	Ἡ ΕΝΑΝΘΡΩΠΗΣΙΣ ΤΟΥ ΘΕΟΥ.

The passage from St. John i. 14, Ὁ λογος σαρξ εγενετο και εσκηνωσεν εν ἡμιν, gives 2774. Clem. Al. speaks of Christ as ΑΡΧΙΚΩΤΑΤΟΣ ΛΟΓΟΣ = 2775.

2812	37 × 76	Ὁ ΩΝ Ὁ ΠΑΝΤΟΚΡΑΤΩΡ.
		ΥΙΟΣ ΤΟΥ ΠΑΝΤΟΚΡΑΤΟΡΟΣ.
2849	37 × 77	Ὁ ΘΕΟΣ ΤΩΝ ΙΟΥΔΑΙΩΝ.
		Ὁ ΧΡΙΣΤΟΣ Ὁ ΒΑΣΙΛΕΥΣ ΕΙΡΗΝΗΣ.
2886	37 × 78	ΧΡΗΣΤΟΣ ΣΩΤΗΡ—Good Saviour.
		ΤΟ ΧΑΡΑΓΜΑ ΤΟΥ ΚΥΡΙΟΥ.
2923	37 × 79	Ὁ ΧΡΙΣΤΟΣ, ΛΟΓΟΣ ΚΥΡΙΟΥ.
		ΠΡΩΤΟΣ ΛΟΓΟΣ ΚΥΡΙΟΥ.
2960	37 × 80	ΥΙΟΣ ΤΟΥ ΑΝΘΡΩΠΟΥ. The autonymous Name of Jesus.
		Ὁ ΚΥΡΙΟΣ Ὁ ΡΥΟΜΕΝΟΣ ΕΚ ΣΙΩΝ.
		ΧΡΙΣΤΟΣ ΥΙΟΣ ΚΥΡΙΟΣ.
		ἡ περιστερα του Ιωαννου.
2997	37 × 81	Ὁ ΣΩΤΗΡ ΤΟΥ ΓΕΝΟΥΣ ΔΑΒΙΔ.
		Ἡ ΣΩΤΗΡΙΑ ΤΟΥ ΚΟΣΜΟΥ.
		Ὁ ΚΥΡΙΟΣ ΤΗΣ ΣΩΤΗΡΙΑΣ.
3034	37 × 82	ΓΕΩΜΕΤΡΙΑ ΤΟΥ ΚΥΡΙΟΥ.
3071	37 × 83	Ὁ ΧΡΙΣΤΟΣ ΤΟΥ ΠΑΤΡΟΣ.
		Ἡ ΘΥΡΑ ΤΩΝ ΠΡΟΒΑΤΩΝ. The Door of the sheep. Epithet of Christ. St. John x. 8.
		ΑΥΤΟΦΩΣ (ΚΟΣΜΟΥ). Greg. Naz.
3108	37 × 84	ΣΩΤΗΡΙΟΝ ΤΟΥ ΚΟΣΜΟΥ.
3293	37 × 89	Ἡ ΑΡΧΗ ΚΑΙ ΤΟ ΤΕΛΟΣ ΤΟΥ ΚΟΣΜΟΥ.

Appendix.

3330   37 × 90   ΚΥΡΙΟΣ ΤΩΝ ΚΥΡΙΩΝ.   (*cf.* Rev. xix. 16 = κυριος κυριων.)
                        ΛΟΓΟΣ ΠΡΩΤΟΣ ΚΑΙ ΕΣΧΑΤΟΣ.

3441   37 × 93   ΘΕΟΣ ΤΩΝ ΖΩΝΤΩΝ.

3700   37 × 100   ‛Ο ΧΡΙΣΤΟΣ ΤΟ ΠΑΣΧΑ ΗΜΩΝ — Christ our Passover.
                      ‛Ραββι των δωδεκα αποστολων.

4255   37 × 115   ‛Ο ΠΡΩΤΟΤΟΚΟΣ ΤΩΝ ΝΕΚΡΩΝ.   Epithet of Christ. Rev. i. 5.

4440   37 × 120   ‛Η ΕΚΚΛΗΣΙΑ ΤΟΥ ΚΥΡΙΟΥ ΙΗΣΟΥ ΧΡΙΣΤΟΥ.

4588   37 × 124   ‛Ο ΑΡΧΩΝ ΤΩΝ ΒΑΣΙΛΕΩΝ ΤΗΣ ΓΗΣ.   Epithet of Christ. Rev. i. 5.

6216   37 × 168   (or 7 × 888 = Ιησους)
                      ΙΗΣΟΥΣ ΧΡΕΙΣΤΟΣ ΘΕΟΥ ‛ΥΙΟΣ ΣΩΤΗΡ ΣΤΑΥΡΟΣ.
                      (The full text of the Sibylline Acrostic of the Ιχθυς, *see* p. 53.)

APPENDIX D.

ΜΕΤΑΚΥΒΟΝ = 888.

Schema of the Numbers of Jesus.

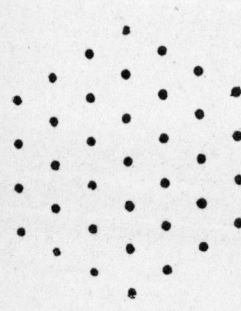

The Schema represents by a series of points the symmetric aspect of a Cube in flat projection. Each point represents one of the Sixty-four constituent Cubes in a cube of $4 \times 4 \times 4$, and of these lesser cubes there are visible Thirty-seven, and never more than Thirty-seven can be seen at any one time. The whole 64 stand for the absolute Truth—ΑΛΗΘΕΙΑ = 64 — and the 37 thus symbolise Revealed Truth, of which the Holy Names founded upon this number are types.

Of these Names the chief one is ΙΗΣΟΥΣ (Jesus) = 888 or 37×24, and this value may be taken as the total value in the enumeration of the figure counting each point as 24. The hidden or back part of the cube shews upon its surface a further 19 cubes, making a total of $37 + 19$ or 56 for the surface cubes. Multiply, as before, by 24, and 19×24 gives 456 the number of ΜΗΤΗΡ (the Mother), and the same number is found by counting only the points within the outer ring of the Schema. From the central One are first generated the Seven (first ring and centre): next a ring of Twelve, making with the centre Thirteen, and all together make the 19.

Appendix. 75

And from the 19 are formed the 37, or as we may now interpret the figure, from the 456 ΜΗΤΗΡ proceed the 888 ΙΗΣΟΥΣ. And we may follow out the imagery of number and form in its gradual development for the unfolding of the doctrinal teaching of the Gematria step by step as here indicated.

In Gematria.

1st Ring . . 6 × 24 = 144 ΑΒΡΑΜ (Abram). Father of Israel.
'Η ΕΚΛΟΓΗ. The Choice or Election. Ep. Rom. xi. 7, etc.

(The 144 or 12 × 12 are a figure of Israel, the Chosen Seed.)

1st Ring and Centre . . 7 × 24 = 168 ΕΠΑΓΓΕΛΜΑ. The Promise. II. Pet. iii. 13.

2nd Ring and Centre . . 13 × 24 = 312 ΑΓΓΕΛΟΣ. The Angel.

3rd Ring . . 18 × 24 = 432 ΚΑΤΑΒΟΛΗ. Conception. Heb. xi. 11.

3rd Ring and Centre . . 19 × 24 = 456 ΜΗΤΗΡ. The Mother. (The 1st and 2nd Rings give the same number.)

1st and 3rd Rings . . 24 × 24 = 576 ΠΝΕΥΜΑ. The Spirit—by Whom was the Incarnation.
ΠΑΣΑ ΕΚΚΛΗΣΙΑ.
ΠΑΡΑΘΗΚΗ ΙΣΡΑΗΛ.
ΑΓΓΕΛΟΣ ΑΛΗΘΕΙΑΣ.

1st and 3rd Rings and Centre . 25 × 24 = 600 'Η ΘΕΟΤΗΣ. The Godhead — Divine counterpart of κοσμος.

2nd and 3rd
 Rings . . .   30 × 24 = 720   ΘΕΙΟΝ ΠΝΕΥΜΑ.
Ὁ ἉΓΙΟΣ ΑΝΕΜΟΣ.
Ἡ ΜΗΤΗΡ ΑΛΗΘΗΣ.
ΜΗΤΗΡ ΑΛΗΘΕΙΑΣ.
ΤΟΠΟΣ.   Abode of Deity.
ΝΟΥΣ.   The Divine Intelligence.
ΕΝΑΙΔΙΟΣ ΟΙΚΟΣ.
ἹΕΡΕΥΣ.   The Priest (of the Temple of Truth.)
ἹΕΡΟΝ ΙΕΟΥ.

2nd and 3rd Rings
 and Centre . 31 × 24 = 744   ΘΕΟΤΟΚΟΣ.   The Virgin Mother ΜΗΤΗΡ ΝΙΚΗΣ.
ΜΑΡΙΑΜ ΜΗΤΗΡ· Ἡ ΝΙΚΗ.
ΜΑΡΙΑΜ Ἡ ΝΙΚΗ ΠΑΡΘΕΝΙΑΣ.
Ἡ ΑΕΙΠΑΡΘΕΝΟΣ ΑΛΗΘΕΙΑΣ.
ΜΑΡΙΑ ΘΕΟΤΗΣ.
ΜΑΡΙΑ ἉΓΙΟΤΗΣ.

N.B.—$\Theta\epsilon o\tau\eta s$ is an androgynous word in Gematria and the $\Theta\epsilon o\tau o\kappa o s$ 744 is the union of the two principles

$\pi\alpha\rho\theta\epsilon\nu o s = 515$
$\dot{o}\ \alpha\nu\dot{\eta}\rho = 229$
———744,

recalling the Ἡ Ἑρμαθηνη παρθενος of the older Greeks. She appears to correspond to Ἡ Μητηρ Σεμελη, spouse of Ζευς, who gives birth to Διονυσος, whose name is a clever anagram of ΝΟΥΣ ΔΙΟΣ—the Mind of Zeus. The whole conception is one of a pure principle of intelligence in its operation in virgin substance.

1st, 2nd and 3rd
 Rings . . .   36 × 24 = 864   ΚΥΡΙΟΣ ΔΕΜΕΙ. The Lord builds His Tabernacle, which is

Appendix. 77

       ΟΙΚΟΣ ΕΚΚΛΗΣΙΑΣ, figured as
       ἹΕΡΟΥΣΑΛΗΜ — The Holy
        City.
       Ἡ ΠΟΛΙΣ ΑΠΕΙΡΟΣ.
       ΚΟΣΜΟΣ ΑΛΗΘΕΙΑΣ.
       Ὁ ΝΑΟΣ ΑΘΑΝΑΣΙΑΣ. The
        Temple of Immortality
        and of the Resurrection
        of the Spiritual Body.
       ΑΘΑΝΑΣΙΑ ΣΑΡΚΟΣ.

Whole figure of
 the Metacube $37 \times 24 = 888$ ΙΗΣΟΥΣ.
       ΛΟΓΟΣ ΕΣΤΙ.
       ΠΑΡΘΕΝΟΣ ΛΟΓΟΣ.
       Ὁ ΟΙΚΟΔΟΜΟΣ ΑΛΗΘΕΙΑΣ.
       ΑΛΗΘΕΥΟΜΕΝΟΣ.
       ΝΙΚΗ ΚΟΣΜΟΥ.
       ΚΥΡΙΟΣ ΝΙΚΗ.

 The constitution of the Schema shews Six lines radiating from the centre. Each of these lines consists of three points and is emblematic of Truth since
    $3 \times 24 = 72$ ἩΑΛΗΘΕΙΑ. Truth.
United with the central point, they become Four, signifying the all-prevailing power of Truth, since
     $4 \times 24 = 96$ ἩΝΙΚΗ. Victory. (I. Esdras iii. 12.)
Three of these lines yield 24×9 or 216—the cube of Six, in Gematria
    $24 \times 9 = 216\ = 152 + 64.$ ΜΑΡΙΑ +
    ΑΛΗΘΕΙΑ.
Together with the central unit this is raised to
    $10 \times 24 = 240$ ΜΑΡΙΑΜΜΗ. The Gnostic
        equivalent of Mariam,
        who represents the Universal Truth.
       ἩΚΑΘΟΛΙΚΗ ΑΛΗΘΕΙΑ.

Four of these radii give, with the centre, the 312 of ΑΓΓΕΛΟΣ and five shew

15 × 24 = 360 'Η ΝΙΚΗ ΑΛΗΘΕΙΑΣ.

which, when combined with the central 24, gives 15 × 24 = 384, the number of the ΠΑΝΑΛΗΘΕΣ, or Absolutely True.

The Schema will be seen to contain the outline of a Cross whose arms stretch from point to point horizontally. The number of this Cross is

11 × 24 = 264 ΑΛΗΘΕΙΑΣ—the number 'of Truth'.

'Η ΠΑΡΘΕΝΙΑ. Virginity.
= 192 + 72 (ΜΑΡΙΑΜ + 'Η ΑΛΗΘΕΙΑ).

So far the Gematria of our figure has been drawn only from the flat or two-dimensional projection of the Cube. There remain other measures. First let us consider the whole surface.

This is 37 + 19 (or 56) × 24 = 1344 'ΟΔΟΣ ΚΥΡΙΟΥ—The Way of the Lord.

'Ο ΟΥΡΑΝΙΟΣ ΛΟΓΟΣ.

ΤΟ 'ΑΓΙΟΝ ΠΝΕΥΜΑ ΑΛΗΘΕΙΑΣ.

ΜΑΡΙΑΜ 'Η ΜΗΤΗΡ ΙΗΣΟΥ.

Within this hollow cube is the lesser cube of 2 × 2 × 2, giving

8 × 24 = 192 ΜΑΡΙΑΜ. Mother of Jesus.

And if we take the Cube of 3 × 3 × 3, which we get by addiing the 19 points to the 8, we have

27 × 24 = 648 ΜΑΡΙΑΜ ΜΗΤΗΡ.

ΔΟΜΟΣ ΑΛΗΘΕΙΑΣ.

'Η ΑΛΗΘΕΙΑ· ΠΝΕΥΜΑ.

ΑΛΗΘΕΙΑ· 'Η ΠΑΡΑΘΗΚΗ ΙΣΡΑΗΛ.

'Η ΠΑΝΑΓΙΑ ΕΚΚΛΗΣΙΑΣ.

'Η ΠΑΝΑΓΑΘΙΑ ΘΕΟΥ.

'ΗΡΕΜΙΑ ΘΕΟΥ.

'Η ΒΑΣΙΛΕΙΑ ΕΙΡΗΝΗΣ.

And lastly, the solid content of the whole cube $4 \times 4 \times 4$ is 64, so that

$64 \times 24 = 1536$ the final number being that of

Ἡ ΓΕΩΜΕΤΡΙΑ ΑΛΗΘΕΙΑΣ.

Ἡ ΚΑΛΗ ΣΟΦΙΑ ΙΗΣΟΥ.

Α· ΤΟ ΜΕΣΟΝ· Ω. (See Appendix F.)

APPENDIX E.

The Decree of the First Mystery.

Ἡ ΚΕΛΕΥΣΙΣ ΤΟΥ α′ ΜΥΣΤΗΡΙΟΥ.

This phrase from the Pistis Sophia is one which seems to contain evidence of the greatest theological importance. By Gematria ἡ κελευσις του α′ μυστηριον is 3177, which on analysis is seen to be 3 × 1059, the number of the ΠΛΗΡΩΜΑ. It is then a triple Pleroma. Now 1059 is by Gematria the number of the ΠΑΤΡΟΤΗΣ or Fatherhood, a term found in the Coptic Gnostic Books, also of ΠΛΗΡΩΜΑ and of ΜΕΓΑΣ ΠΑΡΑΚΛΗΤΟΣ, and these represent the three Persons of the Trinity, by whose command our Lord descends to earth. And 3177 again consists of

1179 = Α′ ΜΥΣΤΗΡΙΟΝ,
+ 1998 = ΦΥΣΙΣ ΙΗΣΟΥ = The Nature of Jesus,

and the whole is Μυστηριον α′ αληθινον το πρωτον.

The Mystery is that of the Alpha and the Omega, as elsewhere shewn (in text, p. 40, and Appendix F).

The number of the Pleroma is a number of the Geometry of the Higher Spheres. 1059 is three times 353 the Hermetic number, and 353 is $2^4 + 3^4 + 4^4$.

Hence the number 3177 is the ninth multiple of the same trinity of Fourth Powers symbolising the Heavenly Places.

We append a Table of various combinations found in the Gematria of this number. Many of these are frankly empirical

Appendix.

and are introduced with a view of shewing the working of the law governing the constitution of the system by which the lesser units tend by addition to evolve greater numbers accordant with the general law, whose truth can only be demonstrated by the testing of all rational combinations of known or suspected Gematria words, whether such combinations have, or have not, been met with in the Gnostic writings.

To prove this will be to prove the existence of a fundamental principle capable of general application, rather than one which is capable only of a selective application.

Thus, 1059 ΠΑΤΡΟΤΗΣ—Fatherhood.
       1059 ΠΛΗΡΩΜΑ—Pleroma or Logos.
       1059 ΜΕΓΑΣ ΠΑΡΑΚΛΗΤΟΣ—The Great Comforter = The Holy Ghost.
       3177 ΜΥΣΤΗΡΙΟΝ Α΄ ΑΛΗΘΙΝΟΝ ΤΟ ΠΡΩΤΟΝ.

or, 1059
  + 1059
      2118 ΜΥΣΤΗΡΙΟΝ ΚΥΚΛΟΥ (674 × π).
      1059 Ὁ ΜΕΓΑΣ ΚΥΚΛΟΣ (337 × π).

      3177 ΑΡΧΙΤΕΚΤΟΝΙΑ ΤΟΥ ΚΥΚΛΟΥ (1011 × π).

      2311 ΠΑΤΗΡ ΠΑΝΤΟΚΡΑΤΩΡ.
       866 ΑΔΩΝΑΙ.

      3177

      2451 Ὁ ΠΑΤΗΡ Ὁ ΠΑΝΤΟΚΡΑΤΩΡ.
       726 Ὁ ΜΕΣΣΙΑΣ.

      3177 ΜΕΣΣΙΑΣ ΤΟΥ ΠΑΤΡΟΣ ΚΥΡΙΟΥ.
          (or πατηρ Ιησου κυριον.)

Investigation of the Cabala.

Of 3177, as expressive of the Logos or Pleroma, we find:—

3177 Ο ΧΡΙΣΤΟΣ· ΛΟΓΟΣ ΤΟΥ ΘΕΟΥ.
ΠΡΩΤΟΣ ΛΟΓΟΣ ΤΟΥ ΘΕΟΥ.
'Ο ΛΟΓΟΣ ΕΝΑΡΧΗΣ ΤΟΥ ΚΥΡΙΟΥ.
ΑΡΧΕΤΥΠΙΑ ΧΡΙΣΤΟΥ.
'Η ΠΡΩΤΗ ΠΡΟΒΟΛΗ ΤΟΥ ΠΑΤΡΟΣ.
ΤΟ ΠΛΗΡΩΜΑ· ΓΕΩΜΕΤΡΙΑ ΘΕΟΥ.
ΜΥΣΤΗΡΙΟΝ ΤΗΣ ΓΕΩΜΕΤΡΙΚΗΣ.
'Ο ΧΡΙΣΤΟΣ· ΠΑΝΤΑΡΧΙΑ ΘΕΟΥ.
'ΙΕΡΕΥΣ ΤΟΥ ΚΟΣΜΟΥ ΕΙΣ ΤΟ ΔΙΗΝΕΚΕΣ.
ΤΟ ΑΝΤΙΤΥΠΟΝ ΕΚ ΤΟΥ ΠΑΤΡΟΣ.
ΤΟ ΠΑΜΠΡΩΤΙΣΤΟΝ ΕΚ ΠΑΤΡΟΣ.

As expressive of the Holy Ghost :—

ΤΑ ΜΥΣΤΙΚΑ ΔΩΡΑ ΚΥΡΙΟΥ.
ΠΝΕΥΜΑ 'ΑΓΙΟΝ· ΜΥΣΤΗΡΙΟΝ ΤΗΣ ΣΟΦΙΑΣ.

And finally :—

2368 'Ο ΘΕΟΣ ΤΩΝ ΘΕΩΝ (or ΙΗΣΟΥΣ ΧΡΙΣΤΟΣ).
809   'Η ΠΕΡΙΣΤΕΡΑ.
───
3177 'Ο ΧΡΙΣΤΟΣ· ΛΟΓΟΣ ΤΟΥ ΘΕΟΥ.

APPENDIX F.

TABLE

Of the Three Primary Figures of the Μυστηριον,

(1)	(2)	(3)
Tetrahedron	Octahedron	Cube

representing

αλφα	μυ	ωμεγα
A (α)	M	Ω
(primitive form)	(το μεσον)	(primitive form)

The inclusion of the **M** restores the more perfect form of the Mystery of the Alpha and Omega. This is preserved in the work of Rhabanus Maurus 'de laudibus Sanctae Crucis', in which the cross-bearing Nimbus of Jesus carries the letters **A·M·Ω**, signifying the Beginning, Middle, and End (Cabrol Dict. Archl. Chret. sub A.Ω.).

Investigation of the Cabala.

	(1) TETRAHEDRON.	(2) OCTAHEDRON.	(3) CUBE.
Comparative Volumes, as per Table.	10.0	40.0	84·9
or as	1178.5	4714.0	10,000
By Gematria	α = 1	μ = 40	ω(μεγα) = 849
or	⎧ 1178 = μυστηριον. ⎨ σκια και κε- ⎪ νωμα. ⎪ (Irenaeus.) ⎩ 1179 = α′ μυστηριον.	⎧ 4712 = μυστηριον (α′) ⎨ 4713 πεντερημα ⎩ το εξωτερον εν κοσμω.	849 = Ωμεγα. μεγας κοσμος.
Do. in other values.	589.2 = πεντερημα.	2357 = φως· λογος Θεου. (235 = ιερον.)	500.0 = Ενδυμα.
	500 = ενδυμα.	2000 = φως· ενδυμα. (αριθμος του κοσμου.)	4242 = μυστηριον α′ πεντερημα ζα- μα ζαμα ωζζα ραχαμα ωζαι.
	1500 = φως.	600.0 = κοσμος.	⎧ 1272 = ἡ γεωμετρια. ⎩ 1273 = ἡ σοφια Θεου.
	⎧ 1767 = μυστηριον (α′) ⎩ 1768 πεντερημα.	707.1 = √2 × 500. (471·4 + 235·7)	1500 = φως. ενδυμα κυριου.
	849 = Ωμεγα. Ὁ ἀρρητος.	3395 = φως εκ φωτος. (= 7 × 485 I.E.O.Y.)	720.0 = Νους. Ἱερον IEOY.
	400	1600 = κοσμος κυριου.	3395 = φως εκ φωτος.

APPENDIX G.

Cabala of the Cosmos.

The Formative principles expressed by the mathematical powers One, Root Two, and Root Three, are assumed as the Aeons whose operation has been invoked to bring into manifestation the visible Universe. These may be said to determine the form of the Regular Solids and are hence fundamental.

Taking as a plastic unit the 600 of κοσμος, we discover in the Gematria of the Macrocosm and the Microcosm the following very perfect example of this mode of interpretation.

(1) $600 \times 1 = 600 \quad 600$ ΚΟΣΜΟΣ.

(2) $600 \times \sqrt{2} = 848$ or 849 ΜΕΓΑΣ ΚΟΣΜΟΣ (848·52 actual value).

(3) $600 \times \sqrt{3} = 1040$ or 1039 ΜΙΚΡΟΣ ΚΟΣΜΟΣ $= 1040$. (1039·23 actual.)

$\phantom{600 \times \sqrt{3} =\ } 2488 \quad 2488$ ΜΟΡΦΗ ΤΟΥ ΚΥΡΙΟΥ—The Form of God, which by Gematria is also

ΙΗΣΟΥΣ ΚΥΡΙΟΣ ΚΟΣΜΟΥ —Jesus, Lord of the Universe.

ΚΟΣΜΟΣ ΕΣΤΙ ΛΟΓΟΣ ΚΥΡΙΟΥ—'The Universe is the Word of God'.

Κοσμος is the pattern as conceived in the Mind of God: μεγας κοσμος its materialisation in space: whilst μικρος κοσμος is Man, its crown in whom the whole is reflected. And Man himself is created in the Image of God.

APPENDIX H.

The Cube of Light.
$$3375{,}000{,}000 = (1500)^3 \; (\phi\omega s).$$

3375 is 15^3 ($15 \times 15 \times 15$); and by Gematria represents the cube of 1500 ($\phi\omegaس$), since only the first four significant digits are of consequence, and the cyphers are written off.

3375 is related geometrically to 2683—the number of the First Precept, as follows:—

$$\left.\begin{array}{c} 2683 \\ \gamma \epsilon \nu \eta \theta \eta \tau \omega \; \phi \omega s \\ = \dfrac{9 + \sqrt{3}}{4} \times 1000. \\[6pt] \text{or } 1200 \times \sqrt{5}. \\ {\scriptstyle \lambda \upsilon \chi \nu o \nu} \end{array}\right\} \left\{\begin{array}{c} 3375 \\ \tau o \; \mu \epsilon \sigma o \nu \; \tau o \upsilon \; \phi \omega \tau o s \\ \text{(Gen. i. 4.)} \\ = \dfrac{3^3}{2^3} \times 1000. \\[6pt] \text{or } \dfrac{9}{4} \times 1500 \; (\phi\omega s). \end{array}\right.$$

In Gematria it is represented by the Name of IEOY—as Bishop of Light,

$$E\pi\iota\sigma\kappa o\pi o s \; \tau o\upsilon \; \phi\omega\tau o s = 3375,$$

and the Descent of Light,

$$K\alpha\tau\alpha\beta\alpha\sigma\iota s \; \tau o\upsilon \; \phi\omega\tau o s = 3375,$$

which creates the Division of Light from Darkness of Gen. i. 4,

$$T o \; \mu\epsilon\sigma o\nu \; \tau o\upsilon \; \phi\omega\tau o s = 3375,$$

resulting in the First Sphere of Light,

$$\Sigma\phi\alpha\iota\rho\alpha \; \alpha' \; \phi\omega\tau o s = 2683.$$

Appendix.

But the connection with IEOY is also a geometrical one as the area of one face of the cube 33750 is very nearly 4850; or 10 × 485—IEOY.

ΦΩΣ—Light = 1500, and ΛΥΧΝΟΣ—a Lamp = 1350, whilst ΛΥΧΝΟΝ, another form, is 1200.

These three words are therefore arithmetically related in Gematria, as will appear by the following table,

ΦΩΣ	ΛΥΧΝΟΣ	ΛΥΧΝΟΝ
1500	1350	1200
150 × 10	150 × 9	150 × 8

so that they represent the harmonic proportionals 8, 9, 10 apparent in physical law. And the first two are related geometrically, since 1350—Λυχνός is the surface of the cube of 15.00 or 3375. For each face of the cube is 15^2 or 225, and all six faces are 225 × 6 or 1350.

The number of the exterior or surface cubes in the block of 3375 cubes is 1178 = ΜΥΣΤΗΡΙΟΝ, and the metacube, or total number visible to sight, is 631—ΘΑΝΑΤΟΣ = Death. So the Gnosis tells us that Death is but a part, and that the visible part, of the great Mystery which leads from Cube to Cube, from the Cube of twice Seven, which represents the Church of Christ, to the Cube of Fifteen, which, as Light, is Christ Himself.

For 14^3 (or $7^3 \times 8$) = 2744   ΕΚΚΛΗΣΙΑ ΤΟΥ ΧΡΙΣΤΟΥ.
+ ΘΑΝΑΤΟΣ = 631
———
3375   Ὁ ΧΡΙΣΤΟΣ Ἡ ΑΝΑΣΤΑΣΙΣ ΚΑΙ Ἡ ΖΩΗ.

And we may go yet further. Beyond the Cube of Light, 3375, and between it and the next, is the Metacube 721, which is ΚΑΡΠΙΣΜΟΣ—The Gathering-in of the Fruits, and this brings us to the perfect Form of Truth, the Cube of 16, the Square of 64—ΑΛΗΘΕΙΑ, and the Fourth or transcendental power of

EIGHT, the Master's number. And the content of this Cube is 4096, which is ΙΗΣΟΥΣ ΧΡΙΣΤΟΣ· ΦΩΣ ΑΛΘΗΙΝΟΝ —Jesus Christ, the True Light, or ΙΗΣΟΥΣ ΧΡΙΣΤΟΣ· ΛΥΧΝΟΣ ΑΛΗΘΙΝΟΣ, and it is the Altar of Jesus Christ— ΤΟ ΘΥΣΙΑΣΤΗΡΙΟΝ ΙΗΣΟΥ ΧΡΙΣΤΟΥ, whose perimeter measure is 192—ΜΑΡΙΑΜ, and its surface measure ΠΕΤΡΟΣ-ΠΑΥΛΟΣ—1536, who mark the bounds of the Geometry of Truth—ʽΗ ΓΕΩΜΕΤΡΙΑ ΑΛΗΘΕΙΑΣ—1536, and this is the Consummation—the Beginning, the Middle, and the End— Α · Μ · Ω—

Α. ΤΟ ΜΕΣΟΝ. Ω. — 1536.

ΕΡΡΩΣΘΕ.

SUPPLEMENT.

I.

ON THE SYMBOLISM OF NUMBERS.

(WITH REFERENCE TO GEMATRIA.)

Of late there has been manifest a greatly increased interest in the symbolic use of Number, and some dim sense that numbers do in reality constitute a sort of Language of Interpretation.

The numbers so evident in the Sacred Books have attracted renewed attention. Some of these, it is recognised, have an astronomical bearing, being connected with the chronologies, and hence with solar, lunar, and planetary periods; and we may trace the growth of astrological systems to which certain numbers are traditionally attached.

Other numbers are more purely geometrical. To some the dual significance clearly applies.

But the pure teaching and symbolism of numbers, already degraded by the false gnostics, was destined to suffer, in the long darkness of the mediaeval times, further degeneration, and a species of idolatry of numbers has resulted, all sorts of fancied potencies and virtues being attached to these symbols, and magical qualities attributed.

At times these appear faintly reminiscent of the verities they were designed to represent, but more often they are but the false attributions of superstitious vanity and ignorance, the stock-in-trade of the charlatan.

The Church in her ostensible teaching has been but little concerned with the mysteries of Number. What she has put forth has been of the simplest. The Apostolic Fathers in their references to such matters have been chiefly concerned with the refuting of heretical teachers, so that much of what they say is apt to convey, and perhaps designedly so, an impression of triviality and almost of disdain. After the third century the Church becomes strangely anxious to crystallise in human words the essence of mysteries which we are bound to believe she always possessed in another and more recondite form, for the alternative—i.e. that she did not possess them—would leave insufficiently explained the artificial aspect of the theological system to which she adheres and would impair her claim to antiquity in this sense.

The simplicity of the geometric and numerical symbolism as conveyed by the orthodox Bishops in any written treatise is well seen in the writings of Durandus, the XIIth century Bishop of Mende, whose work embraces reference to all the principal features of a church and the simpler numbers connected with them. But the teaching conveyed is almost purely ethical in its application, and seems largely an effort of pious imagination. We might quote as an instance the following:

"Some (churches) are built in the form of a circle, to signify that the Church hath been extended throughout the circle of the world, as saith the Psalmist, 'and their words unto the end of the world'—or because from the circle of this world we reach forth to that crown of eternity which shall encircle our brows."

Or again:

"By the lattice work of the windows we understand

the prophets and other obscure teachers of the Church Militant: in which windows there are often Two shafts, signifying the Two precepts of Charity, or because the Apostles were sent out to preach the Gospel two and two."

The study of the true principles underlying the older symbolism of Numbers is of a very intimate nature and involves a well-founded familiarity with pure mathematical principles in their relation to geometric form, and to the cyclic laws governing the motions of the heavenly bodies. Without this as a *constant guide and check*, any results obtained will be liable to error and to dangerous contradiction. Moreover, the serious student who has investigated, without sufficient mental reserve, the workings of the mediaeval Cabalists, and their more modern exponents, may have much to unlearn ere he can approach the subject with a clear outlook.

There is a fundamental principle which must be stated as a sine quâ non if any research on right lines is to be undertaken. This is, the avoidance of all attributions to individual numbers of a nature or significance wholly or uniquely "good" or "evil".

This is the heresy which vitiates the great mass of literature on the subject, and it appears even in the works of famous Cabalists. There is no wholly evil number, just as there is no wholly "fortunate" or "unfortunate" number, but there are numbers which, from special association, have acquired one or the other preponderant character.

And often the very reason for such acquired significance is lost. A modern investigator of astronomical numbers, the Rev. John Griffith, of Cardiff (who has been working out an astronomical interpretation of the Phaestos Disc), as a result of the careful study of ancient calendars, has been able to point out those cases in which an ancient festal day has, by the secular change and progressive error of the Calendar, drifted away from its original moorings, and remained in the recollection of the people merely as a "fortunate" day — with a number of the common monthly count attached to it.

Now in regard to the Gematria, our guide is of course the general or collective sense of the words accumulated upon any given number by virtue of their correspondence with that particular value. Some progress has already been made in the collection and classification of known and suspected Gematria words. But a great deal remains to be done, especially in the recording of words of negative implication or of antagonistic meaning and of a large category of words which are thought to possess, in addition to their ordinary significance, a secondary and obscure symbolical meaning which their Gematria would tend to make clear. The analysis has however already gone far enough to shew abundant evidence of contrasted, as well as of allied, meanings, the good and evil, or positive and negative, signification being present on the same number, indicating a polarity or balance of opposites.

A number may thus suggest a quality or principle, and at the same time, the defect, or excess, of that quality, and thus the regularity of the interpretation is assured, for the choice between positive and negative becomes the choice between the rational versus the irrational, and the spiritual versus the material combination.

In this way, and in this way alone, is a faithful system of interpretation capable of being consistently applied by the method of Gematria, for were it otherwise, and a significance wholly and uniquely good, or evil, found in the words on any given number, it would be possible to harness together a Divine and an Infernal number.

Their sum would be chaos in the literary as well as the theological sense, and the whole of the geometric structure would be riddled with contradiction. Alternatively, if it were not for this element of choice, it might easily appear that a Holy Name could be analysed into two component numbers, one or both of which might possess a significance exclusively evil, which is absurd.

As an instance of the simple polarity above referred to on any given number, we may take the number 46, on which appear the words

(+) Δικαια (Dikaia) = Justice,
(−) Αδικια (Adikia) = Injustice,

and it will be observed that these opposites consist of the same six letters transposed.

A more subtle contrast is observable in the case of Οινος (Oinos)—Wine, and Οξος (Oxos)—Vinegar, both of which are 400 by Gematria.

A further and very striking instance of this polarity is found on the number 1500, shewing the antithesis between Light and Darkness, thus

(+) Φως (Phōs) = Light = 1500
(+) Ωψ (Ōps) = The Eye = 1500
(−) Τυφλος (Tuphlos) = Blind − 1500

Other contrasted meanings are obtained on two successive numbers. This is sometimes effected by the use of the Alpha, which is the Greek negative, and which seems happily adjusted to this use, for, as has already been shewn, two successive numbers are often to be regarded as two expressions of the same value, the greater or lesser computation of some geometric quantity which cannot be expressed more definitely, as it is fractional.

So we find such pairs as

Δηλος (Delos) = Manifest = 312
Αδηλος (Adelos) = Unmanifest = 313

Ορατος (Oratos) = Visible = 741
Αορατος (Aoratos) = Invisible = 742

In this power of choice comes in a possible scope for the Inspirational element in interpretation, prompting the student in his choice to test all values by the standards of Life and not of Death. "The Spirit beareth witness with our spirit that we are the children of God." Our Cosmos presents itself to us under the laws of Light and Darkness, and between these our spiritual choice is made.

The importance of this choice in these days can scarcely be over estimated, for too often spiritual imagery is accorded interpretation in the material sense, leading to the misapplication of a well-intentioned effort, and thus to waste and to confusion.

II.

ON GEOMETRIC TRUTH.

(EXPLANATORY OF CHAP. I.)

Mere words of natural significance fail to interpret spiritual ideas unless a figurative meaning be added to them. By type and symbol alone can the essence of Truth be conveyed. In myth and parable the poet, prophet and religious teacher in all time present to us the realisations of their spiritual sense.

And not in the imagery of words alone, but in Architecture, and its allied arts, some of the most sublime of human conceptions have been conveyed. Architecture has been the interpreter to man of the Universal Truths, those which express the Mind and Works of the Creator, for Architecture is the witness to the Formative principles which underlie Nature, and speaks of the Immutable Foundations.

And these are expressed in the symmetry of geometric forms, co-related by Measure and Number. Thus Architecture constitutes a higher language adapted to sacred uses.

Now in the Greek Gematria we have what may be termed the *Architecture of Language*, for the Gematria unites both elements, both modes of expression, and in a wonderful accord, since words are therein related in their sense to Number, by their Number to Geometry, and by their Geometry again to Building.

For all Building, whether of Words, Ideas, Figures, or Material Forms, is founded on fixed proportionals which we have termed Aeonial, and these we study under the name Geometry.

As a matter of fact we think in Geometry, for the laws of human thought are themselves geometrical, so that, as Howard Hinton has shewn, even the Rules of Logic may be demonstrated geometrically, the Rational Conclusions arranging themselves symmetrically on the surface of a cube*, and their exact number determined in the process.

The concept of Truth is thus possibly more purely illustrated and more vitally appropriated through the exercise of the geometric sense than by any other method. Pythagoras and his followers were obviously of this opinion. And it may clearly be inferred from the Coptic Gnostic Books that the same teaching was believed to be inculcated by Jesus. Hence in the true and faithful use of Geometric Forms we shall in reality be demonstrating truths more subtle than those of which we are commonly aware.

Geometry is therefore a sacred study, the Language of the Great Verities, and it follows that any language built upon Geometry will contain more than at first meets the eye, and will be capable of a limitless power of expression, because its rational terms are eternal in nature, and infinite.

---

* H. Hinton. *New Era of Thought.* (Swan, Sonnenschein & Co., 1906.) He shewed, by this means one more rational form, not included in the text-books. The first application of the method is credited to Mrs. Alicia Boole Stott, and it is elaborated by Hinton, who shews that a four-dimensional figure is necessarily involved in the process of demonstration, and that this Fourth Element is present in the Laws of Thought.

III.

The Geometric Cubit as a Basis of Proportion in the Plans of Mediaeval Buildings

By F. Bligh Bond, F.R.I.B.A.

In response to an invitation to contribute a Paper on a subject of interest to the profession at large, the writer offers in the following essay a theory which he has for some time past been testing, and which tends in his opinion to explain a principle of proportion found in many mediaeval works for which an adequate explanation seems to have been lacking. Much research and good scholarship will be needed in order to establish his theory and to win it general acceptance—should it be found to merit that reward—but the writer's apology for putting it forward at the present stage of his research is that it answers, or appears to answer, equally the historical as well as the practical and arithmetical tests, and to reconcile in a remarkable way certain doubts and contradictions.

In order to clear the position it will be necessary to state briefly a few well-known facts accessible to students in recent editions of *Gwilt's Encyclopaedia* and in works therein referred to. It appears from contemporary records that there were in the Middle Ages two rival geometrical systems for setting out the ground plans of churches and other Gothic buildings, and these were also applied to their cross sections and sectional elevations. These were:—

(1) A system of commensurate squares:
(2) A system of equilateral triangles, which, when contained in parallelograms, gave a rectangular field or setting.

Our chief authority for these is Cesariano, the sixteenth-century translator (or editor) of the works of Vitruvius. Both systems were habitually applied, and there are records extant of controversies which took place between adherents of the rival schools. The first rule, that of the commensurate squares, is called by Cesariano the rule "a pariquadrato", and the second, the rule "a trigono". The first was adopted by the German architects and became more or less identified with their system. The second seems to have been favoured by the Latins, but it will be well not to be too insistent upon this point in the present stage of research.

THE AIM OF THE SYSTEMS

We now begin to break new ground. The question arises: Were the two methods of planning designed to produce results of a different nature, or were they meant to yield effects approximately similar? The question is of crucial importance, and its answer implies also the solution of some obscure points of mediaeval planning, and the discovery of the principle at stake in these bitter controversies.

WHAT WAS THIS PRINCIPLE?

In the writer's view, it was one of geometrical perfection, the object being the reproduction of the form of the Rhombus of two equilateral triangles in the greatest degree of accuracy consonant with practical methods of building and harmonious scales of measurement. As to the motive which led the ancients to their preference for geometric truth—that is another question. For the moment we are on safe ground in accepting it as an axiom of their system that they did work where possible on geometric lines, and that from very early times a peculiar respect—even a sanctity—attached to those proportionals which most clearly accorded with the mathematical principles known to Master Masons.

From this it will be inferred that the contest was one

between principle and compromise, the rule "a trigono" being the use of the purist school, and that "a pariquadrato" of the practical builders. The "German" school, logical and practical, preferred to work on a system wherein the measures of length and breadth were commensurate or uniform, whilst their idealist opponents saw in this something approaching a profane disregard of principles instilled into their guilds by the teaching of a tradition so old, so venerable, that to depart from it was architectural heresy. But even they must have perceived and found by experience a limit of possibility in practical working, and hence in Cesariano we find in the instance he gives of the designing of the Cathedral of Milan a reconciliation of the two ideals.

THE RHOMBUS OR VESICA

Readers are referred to Gwilt (Ch. IV. sec. 3) for an exposition of this highly symbolic feature, based upon the construction given by Euclid in his first proposition. Among all the select proportionals used by the old builders, this, the ratio of length to breadth in the double triangle, seems to stand apart in a position of pre-eminence. Not only do we find it reproduced in many approximations in the plans of our own and continental churches, but it is notoriously used in Gothic detail wherever the architectural expression of the best periods reaches its highest point. And its association with certain parts of a church and with statuary of a certain order leaves no doubt of its symbolic intent.

Modern writers have discovered and chronicled many examples of these proportionals in our mediaeval plans. Notably Kerrich, in his communications to the Society of Antiquaries in the second decade of the last century, has furnished us with material for reference, and following him comes Professor Cockerell with his analysis of the works of William of Wykeham, in which the rule "a pariquadrato" seems to find expression, seeing that the ratio he employs is the

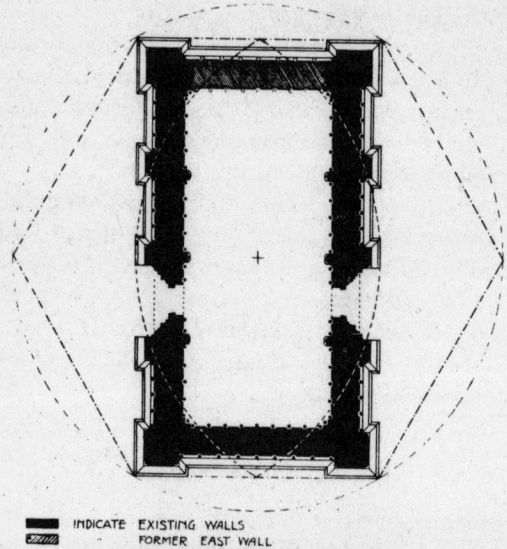

Glastonbury Abbey, Somerset: Chapel of St. Mary the Virgin. Plan showing Rhombic proportions.

most practical of all, and the one which least truly approximates to the ideal proportions of the double triangle, though in buildings of lesser size it would be near enough to exemplify that principle. This is the ratio of Four in breadth to Seven in length. This we will call the "Masons' Convention."

The English Perpendicular, in which William of Wykeham worked, was in some respects a reversion to practical principles, though it must not be assumed that the scheme of symbolic representation by number and proportion, into which Durandus gives us a guarded insight, was superseded by the later builders altogether. It probably tended with time to become over-elaborate, and for that very reason a reaction would sooner or later be inevitable, by which processes of simplification would assert themselves.

To find the geometrical principle in its more perfect expression an examination must be made of the works of the best period, that is to say, the time when architectural achievement had reached its highest point and decadence had not set in. This would be the twelfth century and the early thirteenth century of English work. And reference should be made to examples of the most careful character and least altered by subsequent builders.

It has been the writer's good fortune to discover an almost perfect example of such a principle in the Lady Chapel of Glastonbury Abbey, a structure whose history would be all in favour of a perfect symbolic expression, since the extreme and scrupulous care used by its builders in designing it on ancient lines is on record. Kerrich alludes to this building and gives diagrams and dimensions, but he was not accurately informed as to its true proportions, which have only been recoverable by careful measurement owing to the violence to which the building has been subjected and its consequent partial collapse in width at one end. A plan of this chapel is given, from which it will be seen that the figure of the Vesica is present in a form so nearly accurate as to leave only the most insignificant margin of error, and the figure is repeated in duplicate on the main axis.

THE GEOMETRIC RATIO

The true proportion of the double triangle is as 1 in breadth to the square root of 3 in length, or as $1 : 1\cdot73205$. A building 40 feet in breadth would thus have a proportionate length of $69\cdot282$ feet or, say, 69 feet 4 inches.

St Mary's Chapel has a width, measured on the west face, of 40 feet 1 inch, but as some of the joints have opened it may be taken to have been intended originally for 40 feet. This is the measurement outside the plinth of the angle turrets. In the length there is another open joint to be allowed for, and for this we must deduct nearly an inch. The present measurement is 69 feet 7 inches, and with the corresponding deduction comes to 69 feet 6 inches. If the conventional 4 to 7 had been employed, it must have been about 6 inches longer.

But the inner measurement, which is the breadth between the buttress faces on centre of north and south walls, is computed to have been as nearly as possible 37 feet, and hardly even now deviates from that figure. The proportionate length brings us in this case to the face of the west wall at the level of the cill beneath the recessed wall-arcade, and this is the most natural point from which to calculate a dimension of length.

Although the corresponding line on the east wall is now missing, owing to the removal of the central section for the inclusion of the Galilee—which was done in the fourteenth century—the evidence of the original length of the chapel is attested clearly enough by the remaining data.

The superior accuracy of the inner Rhombus, which is, after all, the measurement of the actual framework of the walling, gives us a suggestion of another and closer approximation to truth than the "Masons' Convention" first described. This nearer approach is represented by the ratio 37:64.

Allusion may here be made to a remarkable fact noted constantly by the writer in his measurements of the various parts of the fabric of Glastonbury Abbey and that of the other foundations and walls discovered. It is that the whole scheme of the Abbatial church and buildings appears to be planned upon a series of commensurate squares of 37 feet, or more accurately speaking, of twice 37, that is, 74 feet. The west wall of St Mary's Chapel marks the western limit of this great series of squares, which are figured in a plan contributed to the *Somerset Archaeological Society's Proceedings* for 1913. The reason for the choice of this number of feet (or inches) as the unit of general measurement is still under investigation and will take some time to determine, as it is by no means clear that some second standard of measure, different from the English foot or yard, was not employed, such as the ell of 37 inches, which was used at Gloucester as a land measure, and may have been used also by the Glastonbury builders.

But this is a digression from the main issue. We have now two approximations to a geometric rule: one rough, but extremely simple and convenient (4 : 7), capable of lending itself to the making of handy builders' measuring rods, and the second a finer adjustment but inferior in convenience, since 37 inches is a long scale, and a relatively clumsy one to deal with,* the compensating feature in this case being that the longer proportional 64 is capable of sub-division by repeated bisection to an extent which would surely have commended itself to the practical mason.

OTHER APPROXIMATIONS

We may now enquire what other fractions will yield us good conventional working elements for the setting out of buildings to the rhombic proportion? In what other manner could the architects of the former time have divided their measuring rods so as to secure the desired result without undue difficulty or inconvenience? There are several fractions giving a near approximation to truth, but only one or two which could be called convenient. The best of these is the ratio 26 to 15, which is alluded to in a work which will be found in the R.I.B.A. Library, entitled *The Canon—An Exposition of the Pagan Mystery perpetuated in the Cabala as the Rule of all the Arts* (London: Elkin Mathews, 1897). This work, being very mystical and ill-arranged, is not freely consulted, but it is evident that the author was well read in his subject and has been most painstaking in his collection of evidence on such points as connect the ancient rules of building with geometrical symbolism. We gather from his pages that he considers that the ratio 26 : 15 was well known and of high repute among the ancients in some such connection as the tradition inherited by the mediaeval builders from remoter

* In the Gloucester records it is viewed as a yard-and-an-inch, or thumb, and spoken of as "virga cum pollice interposito".

antiquity would point out. The Louvre Cubit of 28 digits, unequally divided as 13 : 15, might suggest a practical application of this principle.

We have yet, however, to find proof of the use of these proportionals either in the known history of our building measures or as evidenced in the masonry of our own schools of builders. But this may well be due, as regards the last-mentioned, to a want of definiteness in research. It is a point which would clearly have easily eluded any investigation not based upon the *a priori* conception of the existence and use of such a proportional. In this respect it is hoped that the present essay may stimulate research.

But another and very fair adjustment of scales to integral number in inches offering a near approach to the rhombic ratio is that of 11 to 19—with its complementary ratio 19 to 33. Take 33 inches as your "yard", and the cross measure 19 inches, which we may describe as a "cubit", and you have a very workable pair of measures, since 19 inches is 18 + 1, and 11 inches is 12 − 1. We do not say that there is any warrant for the assumption that such a pair of measures was actually in use, but in all these cases it is well to remember that the masons were undoubtedly in the constant habit of halving, doubling, or otherwise devising simple and compound fractions of their normal standards, and indeed, our own foot of 12 inches is a case in point, seeing that it is one-third of the real standard, that is to say, of the yard. And in this connection it is sufficiently clear that a cubit was often employed which was $1\frac{1}{2}$ feet in length, or half a yard, whilst there is also evidence of an 11-inch foot.†

THE GEOMETRIC CUBIT

The title chosen for this Paper must now be justified. We

---

† The ratio 2x19 : 3x11 (38 : 33) also subsists in our land measures as it is the ratio of the nautical mile to the statute mile (2026·67 yards : 1,760 yards).

are dealing with a proportional which, as already shown, bears to the 12-inch foot the approximate relation of $\sqrt{3} : 1$. Theoretically it is the Mean Proportional between the foot and the yard, but in practice it could not be so if any arithmetical convention were used for harmonising it with the other standards, since any artificial adjustment, if it increased the difference between the foot and the geometric mean, must correspondingly decrease that which lies between this mean measure and the yard, and *vice versa*. In this case the proportionals would appear as:

Foot	Cubit	Yard
4 :	7 :	12

Hence greater accuracy would be desirable. There is a triplet of measures to be kept in reasonable harmony. Our yard and foot are ancient measures—so ancient, indeed, that the mere statement of their probable antiquity is apt to excite scepticism. But the fact remains that they are in close geometrical relation with the principal measure employed by the builders of antiquity—*i.e.*, the cubit of 7 palms; and if this geometrical relation be admitted, then they may be claimed to have been in all probability the original standard from which that cubit was derived, seeing that they do, as a matter of fact, happen to be in the strictest sense of the word geometrical measures—that is to say, measures of the earth's axis. For it has been stated on good authority that our inch, the unit on which the foot and yard are based, represents within a close approximation a fraction of $\frac{1}{500,000,000}$ part of the earth's axial length. Sir J. Herschel, in a letter to the *Times* dated 30th April 1869, says that the inch appears to have deviated from geometric accuracy by the loss of just $\frac{1}{999}$ of its length. Sir C. Warren, however, in his work on the *Ancient Cubit* seems to regard even this as an over-estimate. In any case the loss is so minute as to be negligible in practice, and the amazing fact is that the standard, if originally derived from the earth's measure, should have been so well maintained. The cubit, which is the mean between our foot and yard, is strictly 20·7846 inches, and is the side of a square whose area is 432 square inches, equivalent to an area of 24 inches x 18 inches.

The prime object of the use of the Mean Proportional in measures would appear to be to provide a Standard of Area, of square form, from which other spaces of equivalent area might readily be derived. There is evidence of the highest antiquity for the practice of obtaining equal areas with diverse proportionals. It is found in the ancient Indian "Shilpashastras", or rules of religious art; and Professor Petrie notes such a custom as controlling methods of the Egyptian builders.* In the King's Chamber of the Great Pyramid are recorded, in linear measure, the roots of the simpler arithmetical values, such as are employed for this purpose. These roots would appear to have been among the more guarded traditions of the ancient builders. In the case of the mediaeval workers, however, there does not at present appear sufficient evidence that their object was the equalising of areas of floor or wall space, but it is more likely that the practice of employing these proportionals had become so interwoven with their traditions, and so hallowed by time and religious association, that it had taken on a purely symbolic implication. This would be pre-eminently so in regard to the use of the triangular proportions, as the history of the Vesica shows plainly enough.

But, more than this, it must always be borne in mind that a practice of this sort may be grafted on original necessities of the craft, and that the mason, in order to set out his square and perpendicular lines, must necessarily have made use of the equilateral triangle on each side of his base line of standard length, and would thus obtain a third measure which would be the geometric mean between his two principal units of linear measure.

---

* *Pyramids and Temples of Gizeh*, pp. 194, 199, 200, 220, and p. 181 ref.

The triangular ratio does not appear definitely in Egyptian monuments, which rather follow the laws of the numbers 2 and 5 and their roots—the proportions of the side of the square to its diagonal and of the right-angled triangle whose sides are as 2 : 1, and the hypotenuse consequently $\sqrt{5}$, since $2^2+1=5$, the square on the same. Nevertheless, in Egypt appears in later times a well-marked triplicity of measure, similar to our own, the extreme proportionals being in their case the Mahi, or Nile cubit of 20·76 inches (or thereabouts) and its triple, the Xylon, or staff-measure; whilst their unrecorded mean would be as nearly as possible our yard of 36 inches. The tripling of measures had, without doubt, a religious—probably a Trinitarian—significance, and in the choice of the two leading units we may recall the proportions of the first Hebrew Temple, with its single and double square areas, the Holy of Holies and the Holy Place—together, three squares in length. It would be well if, in the case of some of our own unspoilt Early churches, a careful measurement of the floor areas of the nave and quire (often square) could be made, with the object of testing the principle involved, by finding the side of a true square of the same total area.

To revert to our own units of length. A witty Frenchman once said, "If God did not exist, we should have to invent Him," and the writer would be disposed to make a similar observation with regard to our Inch, that, if it did not exist, we should have to discover it—in order to explain the measures of the ancient world, to reconcile their apparent incompatibilities, and introduce any coherence amongst them. For truly our measures would appear the only possible nucleus of a stable system to which these others could be linked, unless we are to be content with a merely physical—*i.e.*, corporal—origin for all. Such human measures are well known and admitted, but their use argues a perpetual variability, and does not logically exclude the geometrical theory, any more than the counting of fives and tens on the fingers excludes a quite distinct geometrical basis for the denary system of notation. (This geometrical foundation can be shown and is of the greatest interest). Some measures are strictly geometric (in the sense of terrestrial measure). Others are in mathematical relation with these (as the cubit of seven palms). Many are ascertained to have a counterpart in the measures of the human frame. The two systems co-exist, blend, and harmonise. But we must make our choice as to those which we deem original, and those which we think derived. In the writer's view the most reasonable working hypothesis is that the Inch, Foot, and Yard are the original series, and the Cubit, a measure of acknowledged variability, the secondary or derived one.

The argument from antiquity is fortified by the facts in the following table, which shows the units required for setting out areas equivalent to that of a given square, with sides proportioned as 2 : 1, 3 : 1, and 5 : 4.

(1) Assumed Original Unit, on the primitive sexagesimal system: Sides.
$$36'' \times 36'' = 1296 \text{ square inches} \qquad 36'' = 1 \text{ yard.}$$

(2) First derivative (for a double square):
$$(36 \times \sqrt{2}) : (36 \times \tfrac{1}{\sqrt{2}})\text{--}unit,\ 36 \times \tfrac{1}{\sqrt{2}} = 25''\cdot 45$$
(Cf. Royal Cubit of Persia, Chaldea, and Judah.)

(3) Second derivative (for a triple square):
$$(36 \times \sqrt{3}) : (36 \times \tfrac{1}{\sqrt{3}})\text{--}unit,\ 36 \times \tfrac{1}{\sqrt{3}} = 20''\cdot 78$$
$$= \text{Egyptian Royal Cubit.}$$

(4) Third derivative (for a rectangle proportioned as 5 : 4):
$$(36 \times \tfrac{\sqrt{5}}{2}) : (36 \times \tfrac{2}{\sqrt{5}})\text{--}unit,\ 36 \times \tfrac{\sqrt{5}}{2} = 40''\cdot 248$$
$$= \text{Egyptian Metric Yard (early form).}$$

These results err but very slightly on the side of excess, the average in each case being a trifle lower in the case of known examples, but, being geometrical, are liable to modification to suit any arithmetical adjustment of scales desired.

The Geometric Cubit.

How small, comparatively, are the differences between them and actually discovered units will be seen by the following table:—

(1)
Yard.
36″ Eng.
36″ Gt. Pyramid
  (Great Step)
(Practically alike)

(2)
Chaldean Cubit.
  25·45 Geometric.
  25·38 Maximum found

  00·07 defect.

(3)
Egyptian Cubit.
  20·78 Geometric.
  20·76 Nilometer

  00·02 defect.

(4)
Old Metre.
  40″·248 Geometric.
  40″·23 Egyptian

  00·018 defect.
  or 00·009 on the half metre.

The Egyptian Royal Cubit was of seven palms, each measuring from about 2″·91 to 2″·95 according to the size of the digit (·727 to ·737). The "Pyramid" palm yields a digit approaching the latter.

40 digits of ·735—or 12 palms=29″·4, again a derivative of the yard, since $36 \times \frac{\sqrt{6}}{3} = 29″·40$.

The division of the Royal Cubit into seven palms seems good evidence of the presence of the seven as a proportional, either as 5 : 7 : 10, or (more probably) as 4 : 7 : 12. The cubits vary from about 20″·5 to 21″. Seven-fourths of 12″ is 21″, and twelve-sevenths of 12″ is 20″·57, which is nearly the Louvre Cubit.

The Cubit of 20·63, found by Professor Petrie in the King's Chamber, seems to be the most representative cubit of this order. These 28-digit cubits are Royal, or Temple, Cubits.

The Common cubit is of six palms.* The European cubit seems to accord very nearly with the latter, and become readily identified with the half-yard of 18″. The Seven stands out prominently as a proportional both in ancient and mediaeval usage. With the Egyptians it appears to have ruled the relation of square and diagonal, since the side of a square is very nearly as 5 : 7, or as 7 : 10 of its diagonal.

We can express this ratio as 5 : 7 : 10
or as 7 : 10 : 14
―――――――
12 : 17 : 24

and the sum of the two sets of proportionals gives us the better adjustment (12 : 17) found in Roman work.

To summarise our conclusions—in the old and mediaeval systems of measure we can discern at least three main standards:

(1) The Yard, with a *senary* division representing the old sexagesimal system.

(2) The Metre, representing the $\sqrt{5}$ and $\sqrt{2}$ derivatives, with a *decimal* devision.

(3) The Cubit, representing the $\sqrt{3}$ derivatives, with the proportionals 4 : 7 : 12, and a consequent division into 28 (4x7), or into 84 (·7x12).

Of these the first is the overt measure in English work, the 21″ cubit being a latent proportional. In Egypt the cubit is the overt measure, and the yard is implicit only, or scarcely to be detected in the monuments. The second, the old metre, is common to both systems, and though abolished by statute in this country since 1439, is still well represented by our *decimal* system of land measure, where the unit is 3″·96 (+·06), giving us the Fathom of 79″ · $\frac{22}{10}$ of a yard. Were our Metric Yard still in use, it may be that our debt to Egypt in the matter of measures would more readily have been recognised.

* Usually about 18″·24. It unites in square measure with the cubit of 20·63, forming a rectangle of 376 square inches, equivalent in area to one square Euboic cubit, and almost precisely 7/12ths of the area of one square Royal Cubit of 25·38 (=644 sq. ins.). With the square "Remen", which is 4/12ths of the same area, we have again the triplicity 4 : 7 : 12, this time in surface measure.

IV.
CEPHAS
The Name given by Our Lord to Peter

Cephas.

THE NAME GIVEN BY OUR LORD TO PETER.

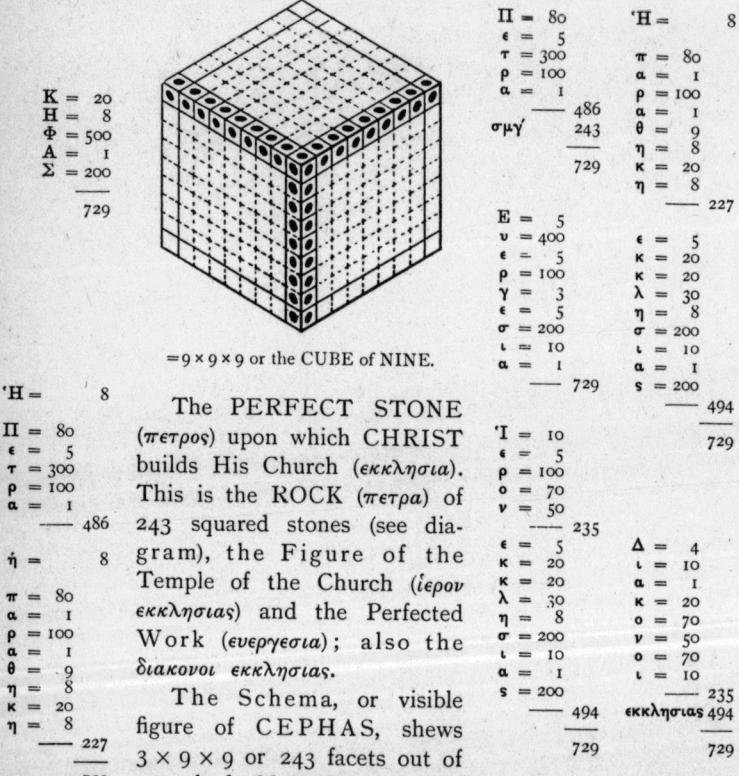

=9 × 9 × 9 or the CUBE of NINE.

Κ = 20
Η = 8
Φ = 500
Α = 1
Σ = 200
―――
729

Π = 80
ε = 5
τ = 300
ρ = 100
α = 1
―――
σμγ´ 486
        243
      ―――
        729

Ἡ =   8
π = 80
α = 1
ρ = 100
α = 1
θ = 9
η = 8
κ = 20
η = 8
      ―――
        227

Ε = 5
υ = 400
ε = 5
ρ = 100
γ = 3
ε = 5
σ = 200
ι = 10
α = 1
―――
729

ε = 5
κ = 20
κ = 20
λ = 30
η = 8
σ = 200
ι = 10
α = 1
ς = 200
―――
494

                          227
                          494
                        ―――
                          729

Ἡ =   8
Π = 80
ε = 5
τ = 300
ρ = 100
α = 1
―――
    486
ἡ =   8
π = 80
α = 1
ρ = 100
α = 1
θ = 9
η = 8
κ = 20
η = 8
―――
    227
    729

Ἰ = 10
ε = 5
ρ = 100
ο = 70
ν = 50
―――
    235
ε = 5
κ = 20
κ = 20
λ = 30
η = 8
σ = 200
ι = 10
α = 1
ς = 200
―――
    494
    729

Δ = 4
ι = 10
α = 1
κ = 20
ο = 70
ν = 50
ο = 70
ι = 10
―――
    235
εκκλησιας 494
―――
    729

The PERFECT STONE (πετρος) upon which CHRIST builds His Church (εκκλησια). This is the ROCK (πετρα) of 243 squared stones (see diagram), the Figure of the Temple of the Church (ἱερον εκκλησιας) and the Perfected Work (ενεργεσια); also the διακονοι εκκλησιας.

The Schema, or visible figure of CEPHAS, shews 3 × 9 × 9 or 243 facets out of a total of 486 on the whole surface. The 486 is ΠΕΤΡΑ (80 + 5 + 300 + 100 + 1), so that PETRA, the Rock, is the Surface of the cube whose solidity is CEPHAS. And ΠΕΤΡΑ σμγ´, or the Rock of 243 stones = 729 = ΚΗΦΑΣ.

But it will be observed that the 243 facets visible belong to 217 separate cubes of which the central one shews Three facets and three rows of Eight cubes each (all marked in the Schema) shew each Two facets. The central Cube represents the Chief of the Seven cornerstones and the triple Divine Potency, whilst the Three Ogdoads of 8, 8, 8, all having a Duality of aspect, stand for the 888 of ΙΗΣΟΥΣ—Jesus, Who unites in His nature God and Man. Each arm of the Ogdoads encloses 8 × 8 stones = 3 times 64—ΑΛΗΘΕΙΑ—a triple Truth, and the whole is 192 = ΜΑΡΙΑΜ, the name of Mary, the Mother of Jesus, here symbolic of His Church. On the further side of the cube, invisible, are 169 more of the lesser cubes, and this is the number of the name of Christ. Ὁ ΑΜΗΝ—the Amen—meaning Truth or Verity, and these 169 cubes, shew again 3 × 64 faces or a triple Aletheia which is Mariam.

$$\begin{aligned} \text{I} &= 10 \\ \text{H} &= 8 \\ \text{Σ} &= 200 \\ \text{Ο} &= 70 \\ \text{Υ} &= 400 \\ \text{Σ} &= 200 \\ &\overline{888} \end{aligned}$$

$$\begin{aligned} \text{Ὁ} &= 70 \\ \text{Ο} &= 70 \\ \text{Α} &= 1 \\ \text{Μ} &= 40 \\ \text{Η} &= 8 \\ \text{Ν} &= 50 \\ &\overline{169} \end{aligned}$$

$$\begin{aligned} \dot{\eta} &= 8 \\ \epsilon &= 5 \\ \kappa &= 20 \\ \kappa &= 20 \\ \lambda &= 30 \\ \eta &= 8 \\ \sigma &= 200 \\ \iota &= 10 \\ \alpha &= 1 \\ &\overline{294} \end{aligned}$$

These 217 + 169 cubes, completely surround and enclose the Cube of 7 × 7 × 7 stones, whose surface has facets 7 × 7 × 6 = 294 = ΕΚΚΛΗΣΙΑ—the Church. Hence the Sevenfold Symbolism of the Ecclesia, otherwise evident in the Seven Corners of the Cube, and the Seven Stars (see text). The Cubes of 7 × 7 × 7 and of 9 × 9 × 9 stones are thus indissolubly connected, and that which lies between is the cube of Eight—8 × 8 × 8— again the three Ogdoads of ΙΗΣΟΥΣ, this time in multiplication. For if from the cube Cephas there be taken its visible surface cubes (217 in number) there remain the 512 which are 8 × 8 × 8, and whose visible surface cubes are the 169 of the ΑΜΗΝ, and their facets 192. And if there be further removed these 169 cubes, there remains the Cube of Seven, whose whole surface facets are the 294 of the ECCLESIA, which is the Trust committed to Timothy—Ἡ ΚΑΛΗ ΠΑΡΑΘΗΚΗ (II. Tim. i. 14).

$$\begin{aligned} \text{Κ} &= 20 \\ \nu &= 400 \\ \rho &= 100 \\ \iota &= 10 \\ \text{ο} &= 70 \\ \nu &= 400 \\ &\overline{1000} \\ &1302 \end{aligned}$$

$$\begin{aligned} \text{Ε} &= 5 \\ \kappa &= 20 \\ \kappa &= 20 \\ \lambda &= 30 \\ \eta &= 8 \\ \sigma &= 200 \\ \iota &= 10 \\ \alpha &= 1 \\ &\overline{294} \end{aligned}$$

$$\begin{aligned} \text{Ἡ} &= 8 \\ \kappa &= 20 \\ \alpha &= 1 \\ \lambda &= 30 \\ \eta &= 8 \\ &\overline{59} \end{aligned}$$

If all Six Facets of the 217 visible cubes of Cephas are counted, the number is 6 × 217 = 1302 which = The Living Church—Εκκλησια ζωσα, or the Church of the Lord—ἡ εκκλησια Κυριον. If all Six facets of the 169 invisible are counted the number is 1014, which is that of the ΣΦΡΑΓΙΣ—the Seal of the Church or of Apostleship —I. Cor. ix. 2.

$$\begin{aligned} \zeta &= 7 \\ \omega &= 800 \\ \sigma &= 200 \\ \alpha &= 1 \\ &\overline{1008} \end{aligned}$$

$$\begin{aligned} \pi &= 80 \\ \alpha &= 1 \\ \rho &= 100 \\ \alpha &= 1 \\ \theta &= 9 \\ \eta &= 8 \\ \kappa &= 20 \\ \eta &= 8 \\ &\overline{227} \end{aligned}$$

= εκκλησια 294